HOW TO START YOUR OWN CRAFT BUSINESS

HOW TO START YOUR OWN CRAFT BUSINESS

BY HERB GENFAN AND LYN TAETZSCH

WATSON-GUPTILL PUBLICATIONS, NEW YORK

Copyright © 1974 by Herb Genfan and Lyn Taetzsch
First published 1974 in New York by Watson-Guptill Publications,
a division of Billboard Publications, Inc.,
One Astor Plaza, New York, N.Y. 10036

Manufactured in U.S.A.

Library of Congress Cataloging in Publication Data
Genfan, Herb.
  How to start your craft business.
  Bibliography: p.
  1. Handicraft—Handbooks, manuals, etc.
2. Small business—Handbooks, manuals, etc.
I. Taetzsch, Lyn, joint author. II. Title.
HD2341.G45 1974   658′.91′745531   74-9817

ISBN 0-8230-2470-9

First Printing, 1974
Second Printing, 1975

To Vicki, Blixy, and Mark

CONTENTS

1

GETTING STARTED

If you're considering starting your own craft business, you're probably already a craftsperson — that is, you practice one or more crafts for fun or to give as gifts. At this point, you now would like to not only develop your skill in a craft, but to make money doing it.

CRAFTS AS BUSINESS

Even if you have a great deal of knowledge in your particular craft, you should consider various characteristics that will make it workable as a craft *business*. Here are certain crucial points to consider about any craft: the amount of money it takes to get started, the time it takes to develop enough skill to make saleable products, the popularity of the craft (marketability), the present competition, and the future of the craft.

Money to Get Started. Deciding how much of an initial investment you'll need depends a great deal on what type of craft you have chosen to pursue. Some crafts, like candlemaking, macramé, copper enameling, and stained glass, can be started on a small scale for a very small investment.

But if a craft requires expensive tools — such as a large kiln or a potter's wheel — you'll find that more money is required. Also, if you plan to open a store or go into a large wholesaling operation right away, more money will be necessary. We started making leather goods with about $1,000, but have always wished we had more capital. Each time we expand, it takes money. Since our own capital wasn't very high, we've had to borrow money several times. So, in general, the more of your own money you have to invest, the better off you'll be. We do know a couple who started with an initial investment of $25.00, but they've kept their craft business small, selling mostly at fairs and at local shops on consignment. Their needs aren't great and they're satisfied to stay small, doing all their own production and selling.

Developing Skill. For some crafts it may be necessary to take lessons or become an apprentice to a skilled craftsperson before being ready to produce saleable work. In general, the more time you put in, the better craftsperson you'll become. However, in some crafts you can start with simple projects and begin selling rather quickly. If you're just beginning to think about selling your crafts, we suggest starting with small, simple projects where your chance of success will be greater. For instance, in leather, a simple hair barrette or belt would be better than trying to make a handbag or hat. Often you can get information from the place where you buy supplies. American Handicrafts and Tandy Leather have all sorts of kits, instructions, patterns, and project books on a variety of crafts. Libraries and bookstores offer scores of books on how to do almost every type of craft.

If you're already skilled in a craft, your first step in marketing is to find out which of your craft items sells best. Although you'll have a head start in knowing your craft, you'll still have to learn how to shape it up into a craft business.

Marketability. This is an extremely important factor when turning a hobby into a business. You may be the world's master ivory fondue fork carver, but if nobody wants ivory fondue forks, you won't have a very successful business. So before you start a business, look around. Go to craft fairs, craft galleries, boutiques, and gift shops, and see what's selling in your part of the country. You may make a business out of selling an obscure craft to a few people, but your chances are probably better if your craft is one that's popular. We say *probably* because there are also problems with an "in" craft. For one thing, everybody's doing it. How long interest in the craft will last is another factor to consider. So you not only want something that's "in," but also something that's here to stay for awhile — and, hopefully, something that everyone isn't making at summer camp.

Competition. Competition was briefly mentioned under marketability, but it's important enough to be considered separately. Some crafts seem to hit such peaks of popularity that it's extremely difficult for a new craftsperson to enter them. For instance, hand-stamped latigo leather is so "in" today that bag manufacturers are imitating the look in plastic. There are huge factories turning out handcrafted latigo belts and handbags for sale to department stores, chains, and discount stores throughout the country. This is competition the small craftsperson can't compete with. The craftsperson who makes a limited number of items is wiser to stick with some other leather look, such as handcarving, and sell to the small leather or gift shop where people are looking for original, well-made items. The fad may pass, but leather itself will probably always be popular enough to support the individual leather craftsperson. The factories will switch over to something new, like denim.

So, observe not only what's selling best in your market area, but also how many others are selling it. If you plan to sell at craft fairs, go to a few. If you're interested in selling pottery, how many potters are at each fair? What is their ratio to the other craftspeople? Is your particular work so unusual and competitively enough priced that it won't matter how many others there are?

Future of Your Craft. Does your craft have a future? This is a difficult question to answer. You can look back to see how old the craft is, how many times it's died out and been revived, etc., but nobody knows for sure how long it will last. A craft that is not only decorative but is also useful will probably have a better chance of survival. For instance, you can always use a set of mugs or bowls, a pair of sandals, a hand carved chair, a candle, a candleholder, or an enameled dish. Jewelry for men and women, in one form or another, has been with us for a long time and probably will remain so. But how long will people pay money for hand painted stones or stained-glass window ornaments? There will probably always be some people who will want them, but will there be enough for a profitable business?

One way to be prepared for changes in market popularity is to always be learning new developments of your craft, designing new items, and experimenting with new materials. Another way is to carefully develop long-term customers who come back year after year because they know and love your work. However, be alert and ready to change with the times if necessary.

GETTING DOWN TO WORK

Now that you've decided that your craft is worth turning into a business, here are some things to keep in mind when you're setting up shop.

Workspace. No matter what your craft is, you'll need space to work. This space should allow you to work in a comfortable position with adequate light so there's no unnecessary strain on muscles or eyes. If at all possible, the space should be permanent. That is, it should be reserved for your work only. You shouldn't have to wait until supper dishes are cleared off to use the kitchen table, then unpack all your supplies, do your work, and pack them up again to clear the table for breakfast the next morning.

It's a good idea to find or build a separate worktable where you can keep the necessary tools and materials ready at all times. If you use electricity, check your space for outlets and be sure to use proper current and wiring. In addition, shelves or space to keep extra materials and finished products is important for neatness and efficiency. Of course, anything dangerous should be kept out of the reach of little children.

Keep your work area and storage shelves neat. Try to clean up after you're finished working, with everything in place ready to start the next day. Having a messy workspace will only cost you time and money, which are vitally important in any business. You won't be able to work as efficiently and you'll misplace tools and materials more easily. Look for ways that enable you to find what you need more quickly. For instance, make a rack to hold tools, use little boxes or bowls for small items, and label containers so you know exactly what's in them.

It's important to have plenty of light in your workspace. If you're going to do most of your work during the day, set up your table near a window or another source of natural light. Otherwise, put up a fluorescent fixture above you, attach a desk lamp, or use another type of light, depending on whether you need overall light or pinpointed light in a small area. You'll find that good lighting will increase your accuracy and enjoyment while decreasing fatigue.

Some people like to sit while they work, while others prefer to stand. If you'd rather stand, make sure your table is high enough so you don't have to hunch in an uncomfortable position. If you prefer to sit, get a stool or chair that's the right height so you can sit without either having to bend too much or reach too high. With planning, you can design the height of your worktable and stool so you'll sit or stand with ease. This is probably the best approach because if your worktable or chair is at an uncomfortable height, the more hours you work, the more tired you'll become.

Supplies. Getting the proper supplies at the right price will be one of the most crucial factors in the success of your craft business. A few cents more or less per square foot or pound for some material may not seem important when you're starting out and only buying in small quantities. But before you realize it, you'll find that your competition is offering lower prices because they have access to lower-cost materials.

So, as soon as possible, you'll want to locate a prime supplier for every material you'll require. By prime supplier, we mean a manufacturer. For instance, if you buy all your tools and materials from a craft catalog that offers all kinds of craft supplies to the general public, you'll be paying higher prices than if you go to each manufacturer directly. Buy leather directly from a tanner whenever possible. Buy buckles from a buckle manufacturer, not a local distributor.

To locate suppliers, ask the telephone company for the Yellow Pages of the major cities near you, plus New York City. (There's no charge for these books.) You'll want to locate the supplier nearest you with the best price and highest quality materials. Write to local and distant suppliers for catalogs, price lists, delivery schedules, and minimum order requirements. Ask for samples or swatches of material, if that's possible (as it is with leather).

Never be satisfied with one supplier; always keep your eyes open for new suppliers because there's always a possibility that you'll need them. If you use only one supplier for a certain item and one day he tells you that delivery will be delayed by two months because he's temporarily out of stock, what are you going to do? However, if you have two or three suppliers available, you can always call another one. We may seem to be emphasizing this point rather strongly, but that's because we've suffered by neglecting it. We were very happy with a particular leather supplier but were caught in a bind when his prices went up and we had no other suppliers on hand. That meant starting from scratch — writing letters asking for swatches and prices, trying out new leather, and finally establishing other leather suppliers. We've found that getting the right supplies at the right price, when you need them, has been one of the most problematic areas of our business. It's the kind of problem you never solve once and for all but have to stay on top of constantly.

THE BUSINESS END

Since you're starting a craft *business*, you'll have to decide what type of business you want it to be — single proprietorship, partnership, or corporation. If you're going to be the only owner and solely responsible legally, it will be a proprietorship. If you want to go into business jointly with others, it will be a partnership. In a proprietorship or a partnership, the principals (owners) are completely responsible for any business debts or losses. That means you can be sued personally for unpaid business debts, and possibly lose your savings, house, etc. Once a business is incorporated, this can no longer happen. But it costs money to incorporate and gets much more complex legally. So, for a small beginning craft business we recommend the proprietorship or partnership arrangement. As long as you're careful to pay your bills and not incur debts you can't handle, you'll have nothing to fear.

Naming Your Business. You'll want to choose a name for your business, and then register this name with your local county clerk: dba (doing business as) John's Pottery, or whatever (see Figure 1). It costs $3 to register this certificate with the county clerk of Tompkins County, New York. Call your local chamber of commerce to find out what the

Business Certificate

I HEREBY CERTIFY that I am conducting or transacting business under the name or designation

of

at

City or Town of   County of   State of New York.

My full name is*

and I reside at

I FURTHER CERTIFY that I am the successor in interest to

the person or persons heretofore using such name or names to carry on or conduct or transact business.

IN WITNESS WHEREOF, I have this   day of   19   , made

and signed this certificate.

....

* Print or type name.

* If under 21 years of age, state "I am .... years of age".

STATE OF NEW YORK   } ss.:
COUNTY OF

On this   day of   19   , before me personally appeared

to me known and known to me to be the individual   described in and who executed the foregoing

certificate, and   he   thereupon   duly acknowledged to me that   he   executed the same.

1.   A business certificate for "conducting business under an assumed name for individual"; that is, for a single proprietorship business.

registration procedure is in your state. This particular certificate is for a proprietorship. It will look slightly different for a partnership.

If you want a specific partnership agreement written up for two or more people, it might be a good idea to get a lawyer to help you. A lawyer can also help register whatever trade name you wish to use. First, he'll make a search to see if it has already been registered by anyone else. If it hasn't, he'll register it in your name. Find out in advance what the lawyer's fees will be for these services.

Applying for a Sales Tax Number. If you're in a state that has a sales tax, the next thing to do is apply for a sales tax number. Figure 2 shows a "Certificate of Authority" that lists the sales tax identification number, name of the company, etc. This number allows you to buy materials and equipment in New York State without having to pay sales tax for them, since they will be used to manufacture items for resale. So, it's very important that you get such a certificate right away, before you buy any supplies in your state. When buying out-of-state goods, you don't have to pay sales tax (unless the two states have reciprocal agreements). But if you buy goods within your state you must pay the tax unless you have this certificate. Simply tell each supplier that you're a manufacturer and have a resale number. Some may want you to fill in a form that they keep, such as the sample in Figure 3. This protects them when the tax inspector looks at their records. It's a little confusing, but in general, any item used in the process of making an item for resale is non-taxable. However, outer shipping cartons, office supplies, etc., are taxable. If you explain your situation to the supplier, he'll usually be able to tell you whether you're purchasing a taxable or non-taxable item.

The sales tax identification number will also be used when you turn in the sales tax that you collected on items sold. And if you live in a state that has a general sales tax, you must collect this tax on every retail item you sell. So if you sell at a fair or fleamarket or church bazaar, you're selling retail and must collect the sales tax. The Department of Taxation and Finance will send you the necessary forms, instructions, and

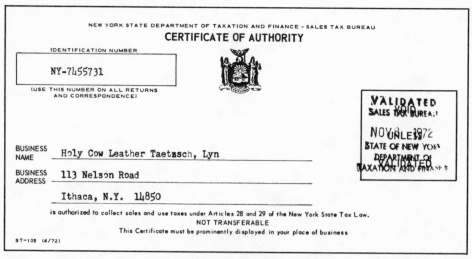

2. *The identification number on this New York State Certificate of Authority should be used on all sales tax returns for tax exemption purposes.*

State of New York - Department of Taxation and Finance - Sales Tax Bureau

New York State and Local Sales and Use Tax

To be completed by purchaser and given to and retained by vendor. **Read Instructions** on back of this certificate.	**RESALE CERTIFICATE**	The vendor must collect the tax on a sale of taxable property or services unless the purchaser gives him a properly completed resale certificate or exemption certificate.

NAME OF VENDOR	DATE
STREET ADDRESS	*Check Applicable Box*
	☐ Single Purchase Certificate
CITY STATE ZIP CODE	☐ Blanket Certificate

The undersigned hereby certifies that he:

holds a valid Certificate of Authority to collect New York State and local sales and use tax.

is principally engaged in *(indicate nature of business)* ....

....

intends that the *(check applicable box or boxes)*

A. ☐ tangible personal property is for resale in its present form or as a component part of tangible personal property.

B. ☐ tangible personal property is for use in performing taxable services where such property becomes a component part of the tangible personal property upon which the services are performed or will be actually transferred to the purchaser of the service in conjunction with the performance of the service.

C. ☐ service is for resale.

D. ☐ shipping cartons, containers and other packaging material are for resale. (see special information on shipping cartons, etc. on reverse side.)

understands that this certificate may not be used to purchase items or services which are not for resale and that he will pay the use tax on tangible personal property or services purchased pursuant to this certificate and subsequently used or consumed in a taxable manner, and that any erroneous or false use of this certificate will subject him to payment of tax plus penalties and interest.

SIGNATURE OF OWNER, PARTNER, OFFICER OF CORPORATION, ETC.	NAME OF PURCHASER
TITLE	STREET ADDRESS
Certificate of Authority Identification Number of Purchaser	CITY STATE ZIP CODE
	PRINTED BY JULIUS BLUMBERG, INC., 80 EXCHANGE PLACE, NEW YORK

3. Some suppliers will want you to fill out this resale certificate and file it with them before granting you tax exemption.

dates on which this should be done. But for now, when you're starting out, the important thing is to collect this tax on every retail sale you make and keep a record of it. It's also a good idea to put that money aside and not spend it, so you'll have it when it's time to turn it in.

Opening a Checking Account. As soon as possible after deciding to start your craft business, open a business checking account. This is important even if you have a sole proprietorship, because it's best that your business monies are separate from your personal monies. Deposit an amount that will start you off properly; enough so you can purchase necessary supplies and pay for them with business checks. In Chapter 7 we'll go into the record-keeping aspect of these transactions. If you have a personal checking and savings account, house mortgage, or car loan at a bank of your own, start your business account there. Tell them what you're doing and they'll show you several types of checks that might be useful. Figure 4 is a sample of one of our checks. Notice that in the upper left-hand corner there's a place to write in the date and amount of the particular invoice we're paying.

SUMMING UP

Now that you've registered your dba certificate, opened a business checking account, and gotten a resale tax number (if necessary), you're all set. You could join the local chamber of commerce or retain a lawyer, but it isn't necessary at this point. One other thing that will be helpful is to put up a sign — on your front lawn or whatever, with your business name on it. Let the world know that you're open for business!

4. In this sample business check note the date and the amount of the invoice in the upper left-hand corner.

CHECKLIST

1. Choose a craft.

2. Learn enough about it to make simple, saleable projects.

3. Prepare a workspace, preferably permanent, with adequate lighting, seating, and storage.

4. Purchase the necessary supplies.

5. If you're setting up a partnership, write or have your lawyer write the partnership agreement.

6. Choose a name for your business.

7. Register your business name with your county clerk.

8. If you live in a state that has a sales tax, apply for a sales tax number.

9. Open a business checking account at your bank.

10. Put up a sign — you're in business!

2
PRICING

Pricing can be tricky, especially when you're first starting out. The main idea, of course, is to make a profit, and the basic formula is *time plus expenses plus profit equals wholesale price.* Initially, you should consider several things. Pricing depends on what type of selling you're doing: wholesale, retail, consignment, etc. You have to know what type of market you're shooting for — a boutique or craft store, a customer at a fair, or a customer in your own store. You must know what your expenses are, and then you should decide how much of a profit you want to make.

In the beginning you may simply want to cover your expenses and the time spent making an item, with a bit left over for yourself. For example, suppose your expenses are $3.00 and it took you an hour to make an item. If you want to make $5.00 an hour profit, then you should sell the item for $8.00; if you only want to make $4.00 an hour, then it will cost $7.00. This type of pricing, however, is a bit simplified. Eventually you'll realize that you can't spend all your time actually making your craft items. You'll spend time selling, bookkeeping (no matter how minimal), purchasing supplies, and developing new products and designs. This time should be figured into your price in the same way as the time spent actually making things, or production time.

As you gain experience it will become much easier to analyze your prices — you can look back at your records after a year or so and see what needs to be adjusted. Until then, the following information will enable you to consider all the pricing alternatives.

COST BREAKDOWN

There are certain basic costs to consider in pricing a product. Specific costs include the actual materials used in producing your product as well as any labor costs (yours or the salary you pay someone else). Nonspecific costs cover your long-term materials and tools, your overhead (rent, electricity, phone, etc.), and miscellaneous expenses such as office supplies or gas and food on business trips.

Specific Costs. The first of these is the cost of the actual materials used to produce your craft item. For example, what is the cost of leather in a belt plus the cost of the buckle, or the cost of clay in a pot? It will be difficult to figure this out by making only one pot or one belt. Instead, use a whole bag of clay or a whole hide of leather, figure the total cost, and divide by the number of items you're able to make from it. For instance, if you pay $30.00 for a leather hide and make 30 belts from it, each belt uses $1.00 worth of leather.

The second specific cost is for labor. Labor costs can be figured easily if you make all your own products. Time yourself — if the product takes two hours and you plan to pay yourself $4.00 per hour, the labor cost will be $8.00. If people work for you, what do you pay them to make the same project? Do you pay by the piece, and do they also get $8.00 for it, or do you pay by the hour? Time your employees to see how much they produce during an allocated period. For example, if an employee makes 20 belts in 10 hours, it takes him half an hour to make a belt. If you pay him $2.00 per hour, your labor cost per belt is $1.00.

Nonspecific Costs. The cost of long-term materials and tools are difficult to break down per item. For instance, the cost of dye per leather item is included in this category. Items such as glazes, kilns, tools, glue, paint, rivets, and nails are nonspecific costs.

Overhead covers items such as rent and utilities for your business. Even if your business is part of your home, figure on a part of your rent or mortgage payment as a business expense. For example, if you use one-fifth of your apartment for business and your rent is $200 per month, $40 of this rent is part of your business overhead. Use the same basis for figuring costs of electricity, water, heat, phone, etc.

If you make a substantial initial investment from your savings or with borrowed money, you should consider the interest on this money as a nonspecific cost and include it in the price of your product. When borrowing money for expanding your business, consider the cost of borrowing this money, even though it may be spread over a long period of time.

Miscellaneous expenses include any items that don't fit into the other categories. These might be the cost of gasoline to get to a craft fair and the cost of meals while there, staying at a motel while on a sales trip, pens, letterhead, envelopes, insurance, advertising, packaging, freight, postage, wood for building a worktable, and interest on a loan to expand your business.

Accounting. If you could keep an account listing all your expenses for a year and look back on it, you could figure out exactly what percentage of your costs were specific and what nonspecific. However, as a new businessperson, you'll only be able to make an educated guess.

In general, you should find that the specific costs (the actual materials plus labor) comprise the major part of your total expenses in producing an item. After all, one tool will probably allow you to make quite a number of items before it has to be replaced. The method we use is to allow 20% of the *wholesale* price for nonspecific costs.

However, you might find that electricity, for example, is a major part of your costs in making pottery. You would then have to make electricity a specific cost. That is, if you find it costs you $100 worth of electricity to make 200 pots, you should add 50¢ per pot for the cost of electricity. The point is, what might be a nonspecific cost for one type of craft could be a specific cost (and by that we mean high) for another.

Specific Costs:	labor	$1.00
	leather	1.00
	buckle	.50
Nonspecific Costs:		1.00 (20% of $5.00)
Selling Costs:		.50 (10% of $5.00)
Profit:		1.00 (20% of $5.00)
Wholesale Cost of Belt:		$5.00

5. *This sample pricing formula is used to determine the wholesale price of a leather belt.*

Selling Costs. In Figure 5, notice that we allowed 10% of the wholesale price for selling costs. We did this because we pay sales representatives a 10% commission for selling our products. If we make our own sales, we expect this 10% to be our "salary" for making these sales. Since doing your own wholesale selling takes time, a percentage for it should be included in the price.

If you sell your products at fairs, you should increase the selling costs because it will probably take more time to sell fewer items. You have to determine what your time is worth for packing and driving to the fair, sitting there all day, and then driving home and unpacking. Also take into consideration the cost of any helpers you employ, the cost of gasoline, wear and tear on your car, and the cost of food and lodging. This will probably result in the selling costs comprising 30% to 50% of the retail price.

If you're selling your products at your own store, you'll have a host of additional costs to consider — rent on the store, initial cost of decorating, fixtures, utilities, advertising, salaries of employees, insurance, and losses due to theft. In general, most retail stores double the wholesale price of an item. If our belt had a wholesale price of $5.00, it would have a retail price of $10.00 in a store, and $7.00 to $9.00 at a fair. (Prices at a fair are usually lower because there is high competition and because there is no store overhead.)

COMPETITION

You could forget everything we've said so far and say, "Look, I'll just charge the highest price somebody will pay, and that's that!" To a certain extent, you have a point. If you're the only one creating some fantastically sought-after product, you can name your own price without worrying about costs and 20% profit margins, and make a 100% profit.

The trouble is, you're probably not the only craftsperson — potter, woodcrafter or weaver — in your territory. Most customers shop around and know the going prices. They may like your work best, but if you charge too much they're likely to go somewhere else.

So you can see that competition poses a real problem. You don't want to sell leather belts at a fair for $10.00 when two tables down they're selling for $5.00. But perhaps you used more expensive leather and put more time into your belts. In the long run, you'll have to compromise so you can be *competitively* priced — that is, within the range of similar products in your craft. You may have to cut back a little on your profit percentage, but beware of cutting back too much. If there's no profit in it for you, there's really no point in selling your product.

Alternatives to Cutting Profit. There are several alternatives to lowering your profit in order to have competitive prices. Perhaps you're aiming at the wrong market. If you make high-quality items and use expensive materials, try aiming at higher-priced shops rather than department stores or discount houses. Or if you plan to open a shop, choose a part of town where people spend more money for top-quality merchandise. Gear your advertising campaign to the group you want to attract.

However, if the quality of your product is no better than one that is lower priced, this approach won't work. You'll then probably have to do more searching for lower-priced materials. It's possible that your competitor is buying in larger quantities or has discovered a goldmine of a supplier. If he can find cheaper materials, so can you.

Another alternative to lowering your profit is to cut the time it takes to make the product. After all, labor cost is an important part of the total price. If you can figure out a faster, more efficient way to make your product, this might allow you to lower the price while maintaining the same profit percentage. For example, we found just such a solution by investing in a used clicker machine to cut out our leather bag patterns. The initial cost of the machine plus the dies in the long run averaged out to cost less per item than cutting by hand. In Chapter 3, Production Systems and Inventory, you'll find other time-saving and cost-saving solutions.

AS YOU GROW

As your business grows and your experience increases, you'll be able to pinpoint your nonspecific costs more precisely. You may find it useful to start breaking down some of your miscellaneous expenses into specific categories: office supplies, freight, insurance, promotion, interest on loans, etc. You'll be able to see what these items cost you per month or per year. Once you have a more definite estimate, you can figure your costs for pricing more accurately.

Look at the sample income statement in Figure 6 for Carol's Creations. At the end of her first year Carol came out with $3,310 profit, or 16.55% of sales. Since she wanted her pricing to reflect a 20% profit margin, some of her nonspecific estimates were evidently wrong. In her original costing (see Figure 7) she had planned nonspecific and overhead costs to come to 25% of her price, but they actually came to 28.45%, as shown on the income statement. As a result, she had a 3.45% loss in profits. Being 3.45% off isn't bad, because after all, we're talking about an educated guess. Perhaps with this information Carol will be able to reach her 20% profit margin next year.

Cutting Back. One way Carol can try to get that 3.45% out of costs and into profit is to cut back on her costs. For instance, she might feel that 5% was too much to spend on promotion. Perhaps a large part of this cost was the color ad she had printed. Maybe next year she can use black and white sketches or another cheaper form.

She feels she can also cut down on office supplies. A lot of money was spent on a fancy letterhead from a local printer, but since then she's discovered a larger, cheaper

	Cost Percentage	Dollar Cost	Dollar Income
Revenues			$20,000
Operating Expenses			
Salaries	10%	$ 2,000	
Commissions	10%	2,000	
Rent	6%	1,200	
Promotion	5%	1,000	
Freight	3%	600	
Utilities	1.2%	240	
Spec. Materials	35%	7,000	
Nonspec. Materials and Tools	10%	2,000	
Office Supplies	1.5%	300	
Insurance	1%	200	
Misc. Expenses	.75%	150	
		$16,690	-$16,690
Net Income	16.55%		$ 3,310

6. *This end-of-the-year income statement for Carol's Creations shows a net income of $3,310, or 16.55% of sales.*

Salaries (labor)	10%
Sales Commissions	10%
Specific Materials	35%
Nonspecific & Overhead	25%
Profit	20%
	100%

7. *Here is the original pricing formula used by Carol's Creations.*

outfit in a bigger city. By getting a more modestly priced letterhead, business card, etc., she can save a few more dollars next year.

Salesmen's commissions are another possible money-saving area. After checking around, Carol found salespeople willing to work for 8% or 9% commission. If she can get them to sell her line at this lowered rate, she'll save 1% or 2%.

So by cutting back or lowering the percentage rates of these basic costs, there will be more left over for profit. Now Carol can keep her prices the same and still make a 20% profit margin.

Changing Prices. Don't feel that once you put a price on an item it must remain the same forever. The prices of your various materials and tools will probably fluctuate quite a bit during the course of your business. We experienced the price of a particular type of leather rising from $1.20 per square foot to $1.50 per square foot in six months.

Raising all her prices 3.45% would be one way for Carol to make her 20% profit without changing the pattern of her costs. To be on the safe side, she might even raise them 5%. So, if a product sold for $10.00, at the new price it would sell for $10.50. An increase of 50¢ on a $10.00 item doesn't seem like much. It probably won't disturb Carol's customers too much, while it will allow her to reach the goal of at least a 20% profit margin.

	Cost Percentage	Dollar Cost	Dollar Income
Revenues			$20,000
Operating Expenses			
Salaries	8%	$ 1,600	
Commissions	10%	2,000	
Rent	4%	800	
Promotion	3%	600	
Freight	3%	600	
Utilities	1.2%	240	
Spec. Materials	30%	6,000	
Nonspec. Materials and Tools	8%	1,600	
Office Supplies	1.05%	210	
Insurance	1%	200	
Misc. Expenses	.75%	150	
		$14,000	−$14,000
Net Income	30.00%		$ 6,000

8. Another income statement for Carol's Creations shows a net income of $6,000, or 30% of sales.

Lowering Prices. If Carol's income statement showed at the end of the year that her profit margin was 30%, as in Figure 8, she might decide to lower her prices — not that she doesn't want to make too much profit. A profit of 30% is fine if it means she would make as many sales as she would with lower profit percentages.

What we're talking about concerns the volume of sales. Carol sold $20,000 worth of merchandise that year, making a profit of 30%, or $6,000. But perhaps she noted a lot of resistance on the part of many stores to buy her products because they were "high-priced." Suppose lowering her prices by 10% doubles her volume from $20,000 to $40,000. In this case, she would make 20% of $40,000, or $8,000 profit.

We're not saying one step always follows the other. She might lower her prices and still sell only $20,000. But often, a reduced price means more sales. We believe that the lowest price you can maintain while still making a reasonable profit is the best policy. This is especially true if you're in a craft where there's heavy competition and large markets. If you're dealing on a custom-order basis and your personal workmanship is in demand, then you may have more freedom to get higher profit margins.

CHECKLIST

1. Figure out what your specific costs are for each product.

2. Allow a percentage for nonspecific costs.

3. Allow a percentage for selling costs.

4. Allow a percentage for profit.

5. Consider competition.

6. After you've been in business for awhile, analyze your income statement to discover actual cost and profit percentages.

7. Use income statement analysis to plan future prices.

3

PRODUCTION AND INVENTORY SYSTEMS

An important step in setting up your craft business is planning a production system that will turn your raw materials into finished goods in the most efficient manner. The faster and more easily you fill a customer's order, the more profitable your business will be. Inventory systems cover two areas — inventory of finished goods and inventory of raw materials and tools. As your business grows in volume, good production and inventory systems will become more and more important.

PRODUCTION SEQUENCE

Every craftsperson has a production sequence they follow to make a particular item. This is simply the order in which each step is done (see Figure 9). Of course, some steps must always remain in a particular sequence. For example, a belt must be cut out of the hide before any other work can be done, and the design must be stamped in before it can be dyed (to achieve a contrast effect).

However, some steps don't have to be in a particular order. The buckle hole, for instance, can be punched after the belt is stamped, dyed, and saddle soaped. We didn't start out making belts in this order, but later found that this production sequence provided the most efficiency. The first thing you should do is analyze your present production sequence. Does each step follow logically and efficiently? Can some steps be combined? Make sure you're not wasting time in your present set-up.

Grouping. One process in an efficient production system is grouping, or working on many items at once rather than one at a time. It would be an enormous waste of time and energy for us to spread out a hide and cut one belt, bring it to a worktable and bevel the edges, get out the buckle hole punch and punch the buckle hole, etc. It's much more efficient to cut a whole hide or several hides into belts and to bevel the edges of a pile of belts. In this way, the time used while moving to a different workspace, setting it up in a particular way, and finding a certain tool, is saved. Instead of constantly changing the rhythm of our work movements, we can keep a steady pace.

If possible, group your work in piles of the same or similar tasks that can be done at one time. If you use a kiln, prepare enough work to fill it each time. If soldering is a part of your craft, prepare enough pieces so you can spend an hour or two soldering rather than starting and stopping for one or two pieces. Whatever your craft, look for ways to group items together so you aren't running from one job to the next.

In general, the more you group, the more efficient you'll become. If you work alone, however, it's not a good idea to work too long at the same job. Soldering for six straight hours will tire you so you'll be less efficient than if you worked for two hours at a time. So in order to conserve your strength and energy, don't go overboard in your grouping.

Physical Layout. Just as important as the work sequence is the physical production order. In what path do the raw materials move as they're made into the finished product? Are the materials delivered to your front door and carried down to your basement for storage, then brought up to your garage to be worked on, brought back to the basement for packing, and finally carried to the front porch for United Parcel Service to pick up? We've exaggerated to make our point. Hopefully, the physical layout of your business isn't this bad, but there may be areas worth changing.

---

1. Cut belt from hide

2. Cut end corners to form point

3. Stamp size on back

4. Bevel edges

5. Punch buckle holes

6. Tool design

7. Dye

8. Saddle soap

9. Buckle

10. Punch round holes

---

9. *A sample production sequence for making a leather belt.*

No matter what size your work area is, the jobs should move along smoothly without a lot of carrying back and forth. Are your raw materials delivered as close to the work area as possible? Do you have enough storage shelves or racks for work in process so it's easily identifiable and accessible? Is your packing area in the most convenient place for pick-up by delivery trucks? Is your storage area for finished goods close to the packing area? Check out the physical layout thoroughly and see what you can do to improve it.

JOB COMPLETION FORM

If you work with others filling orders for customers, you might find a job completion form useful (see Figure 10). When an order comes in, we immediately make up a form listing the name of the customer, date of order, and amount and description of items ordered. Job completion forms for all orders are tacked on the wall in the workroom, with the earliest date on top.

The original order is put into a folder marked "Orders To Be Typed," so that an invoice/packing list can be prepared for it. By the time the order is made and brought to

---

Job Completion Form No. _32_

Account: __Bert's Shoes__   Date: __1/14/74__

Amount	Item	Tooled	Dyed	Complete
2 Dz.	1 ¾" Belts, assorted			
	4 S, 12 M, 8 L			
1 Dz.	3/4" Belts, assorted			
	3 S, 3M, 3L, 3LL			

10. We use this job completion form in our leathercraft business, but you can design one to fit your own craft.

the packing area, the packing list will be ready to enclose with the order.

When a worker is ready to start a new order, he takes the top job form off the wall. He then goes to the shelf where all the belt blanks are kept and takes the various sizes he'll need to fill the order. (We stock these belt blanks with beveled edges, buckle hole punched, and sizes marked, in piles ready to be used for orders.) He brings them to a tooling area and tools all the belts for this order. Finally he puts them with the job form (after signing his initials under "Tooled"), on a shelf near the dyeing area. The person who does the dyeing simply takes the order off the shelf when he's finished with the previous order. The dyer also signs his initials after completing the order, and places it on another shelf for work that has been dyed. Now another worker can pick up the order and finish it — saddle soap, buckle, hole punch, etc. This person signs the job form under "Complete," then brings it with the order to the packing area. The packer looks at the name of the account on the job form, pulls the packing list, and packs the order.

Sometimes the packer may notice a mistake in the order — perhaps there's a belt missing or a buckle wasn't put on right. By looking at the job form the packer can notify the person who worked on the order so the mistake can be corrected. This helps improve that individual's future workmanship and places responsibility where it belongs.

Job forms will vary depending upon your craft. Decide what the basic steps are in the completion of a product and make a column heading for each one. The workers can tack the form to a cardboard box when they begin the order and keep all the parts in it until completion. The box of finished products is then brought to the packing area. The "Job Completion Form" idea can be molded to fit your particular craft business.

FINISHED GOODS INVENTORY

You may decide to ship orders from an inventory stock rather than using the individual job system just described. This means that when an order comes in, it's taken off a shelf or rack of finished goods. Individual orders never go to the workroom. When stock of a particular item gets low, the workers are told to make more of that item in order to build up the stock.

This method works if you can prepare in advance enough stock of all the items you sell. Naturally you can't stock custom-made items. Keep in mind that if you offer 50 items that come in 10 colors, you'd have 500 items to stock just to have one of each. A lot depends upon whether you allow customers to choose size, color, and material, or whether you have a standard list of styles.

We're presently at the point of trying to change over from the individual job system to the inventory stocking system. We used to allow customers to choose any of our designs and colors, and that made too many items for us to stock. This year we're offering handbags in only two or three colors of each style, and belts in a brown or color assortment only. We hope to be able to have enough of everything so we can ship directly from our stock.

Advantages and Disadvantages. One advantage of shipping from stock is that it enables you to ship orders faster. Obviously, if you don't start making an order until you receive it, you can't ship it immediately. By having stock, it's simply a matter of packing time before your product can be shipped. It's even possible to ship an order the same day it's received.

Another advantage of stock is the elimination of the individual job completion form. Instead of working on different types of items in various colors, a worker could make large quantities of a particular item, design, or color. This will make the work completion process more efficient.

A disadvantage of stocking is the chance that only some types of items will be sold. You may stock 50 of an item that no one ever buys. Probably the best solution is to begin by stocking in small quantities until you see which items sell best. If you do end up with items you can't sell, try having a sale at the end of the year or around holidays.

Another problem with stocking is the large initial investment in raw materials, labor, and storage space that must be made. You must purchase enough raw materials to make a minimum amount of each item you carry. If you don't do all your own work, workers must be paid to make these items in advance. Also, it will take more space to store the items so they'll be easily accessible to the packer. Once you get the system going, however, you'll be able to replace your initial investment with money earned from sales.

Weigh these advantages and disadvantages as they apply to your craft and the size of your business. We found the individual job system to be very useful in the beginning. We didn't have the initial investment or storage space to stock all items, nor did we know which items would be our best sellers. Now, however, we feel that stocking is the best method for us. You'll have to decide which is best for you. Perhaps a combination such as stocking only small items which sell fast might work well at first.

STOCK CONTROL

If you plan to stock finished goods, you'll need some form of control over this stock. If you have just a few items and do the packing yourself, simply note when the number of an item falls below a certain amount. For example, if you make a dozen kinds of pots and keep a shelf filled with each type, you can easily see when you're running low.

However, if you have more than a few kinds of items that are stored so they can't be easily seen and counted, or have several people packing or taking goods off the shelves, you'll need an inventory system to keep control of your stock. Here's one simple method: place a 3″ × 5″ card on each rack or shelf listing the number of items it contains. When anyone removes items from the shelf, they must subtract what they take and write in the new number. Once a day, or each week, have someone check the cards to see which items are low and write up a job completion form to have those items made.

Stock Control Book. For large, complex stock storage areas or for better control, we suggest this method: on a columnar pad for your stock records, give every item you stock a number and place one number on top of each page (see Figure 11). Label column headings for "Date," "In Amount," "Out Amount," "Job or Invoice No.," and "Balance." The original balance should be the amount of each item in stock when you start.

At the end of each day or week, record all the items shipped. To do this, fill in the invoice number, shipping date, and quantity shipped. Then subtract the amount shipped from the previous balance and record the new balance (see Figure 12). On January 3rd, 2 dozen style #42 belts were shipped to a customer on invoice #546. We placed "1/3" in the date column, "2 doz." under "Out Amount," and "#546" under "Job/Invoice No." The previous balance was 64 dozen so we subtracted 2 dozen and wrote in a new balance of 62 dozen.

Whenever a job form is completed and new merchandise added to inventory, it should be recorded in the book under "In Amount" (see Figure 13). On January 4th, 10 dozen style #42 belts for Job Form #22 were made and added to inventory. We placed "1/4" in the date column, "10 doz." under "In Amount," and "#22" under "Job/Invoice No." To the previous balance of 62 dozen we added 10 dozen and wrote in a new balance of 72 dozen.

Periodically, an actual physical inventory should be taken to verify the balances in the inventory control book. Since mistakes will be made, you shouldn't operate too long without correcting the balances to match your actual physical stock.

MATERIALS AND TOOLS INVENTORY

Having adequate control of your raw materials and tools inventory is even more crucial than controlling your finished goods inventory. If you find yourself short of a particular style, you can always make more immediately. But if you suddenly discover you're out of a crucial raw material or have broken the last of a tool, you won't be able to make anything requiring that raw material or tool until you replace it.

On one occasion this happened to us when a snap setter broke. We couldn't set any more snaps until we replaced this tool. Now we keep two or more of every tool at all times. If one breaks, we have others to use until we replace it.

Leather shortages are another problem we've experienced. Sometimes we have to wait three or four weeks for a shipment, which means we have to plan to have a four week supply on hand at all times. To be on the safe side, a five or six week supply is better. There's nothing worse for your business than having a pile of orders to fill and no leather for them.

The point we're making is that you need some kind of system to help you keep track of your raw materials and tools. You may be able to keep it all in your head if you're the only one using the materials. But if there are other people working, you need a way to coordinate the use of materials so you can reorder in advance.

Simple Control System. If you keep your raw materials on shelves, racks, or other storage areas that can be marked, you can use the same system described for finished goods stock control. Attach a 3 " X 5" card to each rack or shelf and write the amount of material presently in stock. When someone uses material, they should subtract it and write in the new amount. Periodically, you should check all the cards to see which items need to be reordered.

For small tools and other items that need to be replaced only when they break or wear out, use this simple system. First, decide how many of each tool you need in the work area. If you need one tool, buy two extra, and if you need two in the work area, buy three extra. Keep all the extra tools boxed in a separate area so no one will use them. When a tool breaks or is worn out, the worker must bring you the bad tool for replacement. When you get down to one replacement of a particular tool, order more.

Volume pricing will also probably affect the number of tools you purchase at one time. For instance, if six of an inexpensive tool cost less per tool than one or two, buy six and store the ones you don't need. The number of extra tools you buy depends on how much cash you have to spare and the rate at which the tools are used up or broken.

Stock Control Book. This book is set up similarly to the one for finished goods

Style No. _____

Date	In Amount	Out Amount	Job or Invoice No.	Balance

11. This page from a stock control book shows how to set up columns and enter the initial balance.

Style No. _____

Date	In Amount	Out Amount	Job or Invoice No.	Balance
				64 DZ.
1/3		2 DZ.	546	

12. A page from a stock control book shows how a shipment to a customer is recorded.

Style No. _____

Date	In Amount	Out Amount	Job or Invoice No.	Balance
				64 DZ.
1/3		2 DZ.	546	62 DZ.
1/4	10 DZ.		22	72 DZ.

13. The same page from a stock control book, but with an additional entry made when more finished goods are added to the inventory.

except that you'll also need a stock use list. You won't be able to tell from filled orders how much stock was used, so workers should make a note on the list when they take something. At the end of the day or week you'll use the list to record the "Stock Out" amounts.

The stock use list (Figure 14) shows that when John took four hides of yellow 8/9 latigo, he listed the date, his name, the item, and the amount taken. When Carol took a new mallet out of stock she listed it in a similar way. It's important here to keep your stock of supplies in a separate area from the workspace and to be certain every worker lists each item taken from stock.

In the stock control book (see Figure 15) we entered "1/8" under the date, "John" under "Name," "4" under "Stock Out." The previous balance was 15 so we subtracted 4 and wrote in the new balance of 11. Next, we recorded a shipment that came in that day. The date is the same. Under "Name" we wrote "Herman," the name of our supplier and under "Stock In" we wrote "50," the number of hides received. We added the 50 to the previous balance of 11 and wrote in 61.

All these systems will be valuable only if they're used properly. All workers must record each item taken or delivered. The control books must be looked at periodically so orders can be placed for items that are low in stock. A decision should be made ahead of time as to when you plan to reorder, that is, when the balance gets below a certain number.

WHY HAVE SYSTEMS?

All of this may seem elaborate and indeed, it's a bit more paperwork than the single craftsperson may require. When you used to spend a whole day making one unique belt for a friend, you wouldn't dream of inventory control systems. But now you're in business and your craft has caught on. People like the look of your leather or your pottery and you've decided to produce in quantity.

If you're selling to retail stores who like the way your work sells, their customers expect a ready supply of your work. Store owners, you'll find, want your goods on their shelves within a week or two after they order. Your success at this stage depends almost entirely on how quickly you deliver.

The nature of a good system allows you to see exactly what you have and need at a glance. It's a powerful planning tool for all the materials, tools, labor, and stock you'll need to have to fill orders quickly. When selling in volume, your reputation depends upon delivering on time, particularly during holidays. You'll notice that many orders have a cancellation date written in. If the stores don't receive their orders by a certain date, they have the right to send all your goods back. It's even possible that they'll give up on you and choose another craftsperson who can supply them as they need it.

Production and inventory systems are well worth the time in planning and in keeping them up to date. If you've heard of a business failing because of "poor management," lack of organization is one of the factors that cause such failure. With other craftspeople competing for customers you can, by using control systems, be the one that makes it and stays in business.

Stock Use List

Date	Name	Item	Amount
1/5	John W.	8/9 yellow lat.	4 hides
1/7	Carol S.	large mallet	1

14. Your stock use list should be kept in a handy place near your stock so workers can easily record what they take.

Stock Item: 8/9 yellow latigo

Date	Name	Stock In	Stock Out	Balance
				15 hides
1/8	John W.		4 hides	11 "
1/8	Herman	50 hides		61 "

15. This page from a stock control book shows an "In and Out" transaction.

CHECKLIST

1. Plan a production sequence for each item you make so it can be produced most efficiently in the least amount of time.

2. Group your work into batches wherever possible.

3. Check out your physical production layout – eliminate any inefficiencies.

4. Design a job completion form to fit your craft.

5. Plan to stock finished goods or use the individual job system.

6. If you're going to stock, set up an easily accessible storage area.

7. If you're stocking finished goods, use the simple stock control method, or set up a stock control book.

8. Order extra, small-sized tools that might need to be replaced and keep them in stock.

9. Decide on minimum amounts of raw materials that must be kept in stock at all times.

10. Set up either the simple system or stock control book for raw materials and tools.

11. Up-date your lists regularly.

SHIPPING, PACKING, AND BILLING

As the volume of your sales increases, many of the stores you sell to will be too far away for you to personally deliver your goods. You'll now have to find an efficient shipper or "carrier" with reasonable rates.

Another important part of your business is the process of inspecting, wrapping, and packing your product along with business forms such as bills of lading and invoices.

SHIPPING METHODS

There are several ways to ship packages: parcel post, United Parcel Service, and truck. The method you choose depends on your particular needs as a business.

We feel that United Parcel Service is the easiest, cheapest, and most efficient method, so we use it whenever we can. For states not covered by UPS we use parcel post, and when we have a shipment over 100 pounds for one customer we use a trucking company. Some stores can't receive UPS shipments, so we keep a list of these stores and ship to them via parcel post.

Parcel Post. This method of shipping is handled through the post office. The maximum weight allowed for any package is 40 pounds, and the maximum size is 84 inches, length and girth combined (see Figure 16).

Parcel post rates depend on the weight and destination of your goods. You can get a chart with this information from your local post office. Packages can be insured for a small extra charge depending on the value of the package. Since insuring the package is the only way it can be traced if it gets lost, it's a good idea if your goods are valuable.

Delivery time with parcel post varies. Our local post office said to expect two or three days for local delivery and six to ten days for New York to California. However we've found that you can never tell what will happen with parcel post. One package we sent took two weeks to reach New Jersey from New York.

United Parcel Service. United Parcel Service delivers to all states except Utah, Arizona, Nevada, Montana, Idaho, Hawaii, Alaska, and Puerto Rico. The maximum weight per

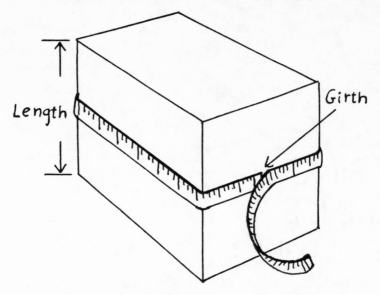

16. This diagram illustrates how to measure length and girth.

package is 50 pounds and the maximum size is 108 inches, length and girth combined. If you have several packages going to one customer, the maximum total pounds per day per customer is 100. That is, you can ship up to a total of 100 pounds to any one customer in any one day.

The cost of United Parcel Service also varies depending on weight and destination. They'll provide a chart with this information based on zip code zones, so you must know the zip code. Packages are automatically insured for $100 but you can insure them for more at a small cost. Unlike parcel post, every package can be traced.

Delivery times for UPS are generally better than for parcel post. Local delivery is overnight, New York to Pennsylvania takes one or two days, and New York to Florida takes four or five days. They also provide an air service from New York to California, Oregon, and Washington, which takes two or three days.

UPS will pick up packages at your home or place of business for a charge of $2.00 per week. No matter how many packages you have that week, the charge is still $2.00. They pick up and deliver only on Monday through Friday. If you have at least one shipment every week, arrange with your local UPS office for a daily pick-up service. After an initial deposit of $50, they'll bill you each week for the $2.00 pick-up charge plus the cost of any shipments. You'll have to sign a contract such as the one shown in Figure 17. They'll bring you all the rate charts, C.O.D. stickers, and other materials you'll need.

Every day in your UPS Book (see Figure 18), you'll fill in the date and list any orders you're shipping that day. The driver takes the original, and the copy stays in the book for your records. This gives you a permanent record of every shipment made.

Truck. Trucking companies are necessary if you have over 100 pounds to ship in any one day to a single customer. In general, trucking companies are too expensive if you only have small shipments to a few customers. We receive a lot of supplies by truck, but use them for shipping out only when we have a large order.

Date *February 28, 1973*

Gentlemen:

This will acknowledge receipt of your check for $ *50.⁶⁰* ,
which you have voluntarily deposited with us. The deposit will be considered
as a prepayment toward four weekly delivery charges.

☒ This is an initial deposit.

☐ This is an additional deposit which brings

your total deposit to $_____ .

Under this arrangement, we will continue to send bills weekly. After
each four week period, the deposit will be re-established by your payment
of the actual delivery charges for such period.

If your use of our service should be discontinued, we will refund to you
the full amount of the deposit, less any charges for service due us at
that time.

Please signify your acceptance of this arrangement in the space
provided below.

Very truly yours,
UNITED PARCEL SERVICE, INC.

By *Robert A. Zolls*

Accepted:

Shipper Name *Holy Cow Leather*

By *Lynn Taitynd*

Address *113 Nelson Rd.*

Ithaca, New York 14850

Shipper No. **NY** **1-26-749** LBS.

U7251 4-72

17. *You must sign this type of contract with United Parcel Service to establish a daily
pick-up service.*

18. *This page from a UPS book lists several shipments.*

To find out the exact rates for shipping by truck, look in the Yellow Pages of your phone book under "Trucking." Call several companies to find out if they'll handle your location and merchandise, and ask what their charges are. Usually there's a minimum charge for a small pick-up and sometimes an extra charge if it's for a single customer. Trucking companies usually handle a limited area, so if your shipment is going far, it might start out on one truck and be transferred to another trucking company.

Ask for delivery schedules when you call, but in general, expect a truck to take longer than United Parcel Service. We have goods sent from New York to Missouri by truck in five to ten days.

FOREIGN SHIPMENTS

We're just going to touch on this subject briefly. Basically, there are three problems with foreign shipments — getting your money, shipping the merchandise, and red tape. In the U.S.A., if an account doesn't pay you there are methods of trying to collect. If a customer in a foreign country doesn't pay you, the U.S. Marines will rarely take up your cause.

To solve the money problem there's a "letter of credit" that may help you. Let's say you're shipping $1,000 worth of merchandise to Japan. The customer goes to his bank, which then sends your bank a letter of credit worth $1,000. As soon as you can prove shipment, your bank gives you the $1,000. For orders of at least $500 or more, you should ask your customer for such a letter of credit, first advising him of the total costs. For small orders, insist upon "payment against a sight draft," which means payment in advance.

For shipping, you'll have to use an overseas shipper, either ocean or air freight. This can be very complicated and expensive.

The red tape involves all the forms you'll have to fill out. Approval by a foreign consulate will be necessary before the shipment can be made. There are all kinds of rules, tariffs, etc., concerning foreign shipments. The amount and type vary with the country and kind of merchandise being shipped.

Rather than handling all this yourself, you can look up a "forwarder" who will handle it for you. For a set fee they'll take care of all the forms, fees, and shipping. On the east coast, you'll find forwarders in New York City. If you don't know where to find one in your area, call your local chamber of commerce or the shipping department of a local industry. If they ship to foreign countries, they may be able to give you the name of the forwarder they use.

Canada. Shipments to Canada are easier to deal with (see Chapter 5 for collection procedures). There is far less red tape because shipments under $100.00 don't require special papers. You can ship parcel post by filling out a card (see Figure 19).

For orders over $100, you'll have to fill out an M-A commercial invoice (see Figure 20) and send it to your customer. He'll have to show them when he picks up the merchandise at the post office in Canada. You can purchase these forms from Unz & Company, 24 Beaver Street, New York, N.Y. 10004.

PARCEL POST CUSTOMS DECLARATION — UNITED STATES OF AMERICA

INSTRUCTIONS GIVEN BY SENDER *Dispositions de l'Expéditeur*	QTY	USE INK OR TYPEWRITER ITEMIZED LIST OF CONTENTS	VALUE (U.S. $)
If undeliverable as addressed: *Au cas de non-livraison:* ☐ Return to sender. Return charges guaranteed. *Le colis doit être renvoyé à l'expéditeur,* *qui s'engage à payer les frais de retour.* ☐ Forward to. (*Le colis doit être réexpé- dié à*):			

☐ Abandon. (*Abandon du colis.*)

(Sender's Signature—*Signature de l'expediteur*)

MAILING OFFICE DATE STAMP	LBS.		
	OZS.		
	POSTAGE $	ACCEPTING CLERK'S INITIALS	INSURED VALUE (U.S. $)

PS Form 2966-A, June 1972

19. You'll have to fill out a post office form when shipping parcel post to Canada.

Form No. 8 (Bond Paper) or Form No. 72 (Onion Skin) M-A 8½ x 14 Size   Printed in U.S.A. and Sold by Uns & Co., Inc., 24 Beaver St., N.Y. 10004

1959 M-A Invoice approved by Canadian Customs (1959) for goods sold by exporter prior to importation, for entry at Most Favoured Nation Tariff Rates.

Place and Date.................................19...   Invoice No.............

Invoice of...purchased

by...of...

from..of...

to be shipped from.................................per...

TERMS:...CUSTOMER'S ORDER NO.............OUR ORDER NO.............

Country of Origin	Marks and Numbers on Packages	QUANTITIES AND DESCRIPTION OF GOODS	Fair Market value at time and place of shipment in currency of country of export (See clauses 5 to 8 of certificate of value hereon)	Selling Price to Purchaser in Canada (Specify currency of settlement)	
				¢¢	Amount

NOTE: the following facts must be shown:

Amount of: Freight, if any, prepaid and charged..............................

Freight, if any, prepaid and not charged............................... *

Freight, if any, allowed to be deducted by importer on settlement........ *

* If any freight is prepaid by the exporter and not charged, or is allowed to be deducted by the importer on settlement, a statement must be made on this invoice indicating whether or not the practice is consistent with the exporter's domestic market freight policy.

(M) I, the undersigned, do hereby certify as follows:—

1. That I am the (insert official capacity)...of (name of exporter)...............................
exporter of the goods described in the within invoice;
2. That the said invoice is in all respects correct and true;
3. That the said invoice contains a true and full statement showing the price actually paid or to be paid for the said goods, the actual quantity thereof and all charges thereon;
4. That there is included in the said invoice the true value of all cartons, cases, crates, boxes and coverings of any kind and all charges and expenses incident to placing the said goods in condition packed ready for shipment to Canada;
5. That the said invoice also exhibits the fair market value, at the time when and place from which the goods were shipped directly to Canada, of like goods when sold in the same or substantially the same quantities for home consumption in the ordinary course of trade under competitive conditions to purchasers located at that place with whom the vendor deals at arm's length and who are at the same or substantially the same trade level as the importer;
6. That where like goods are not sold for home consumption in the circumstances described in the preceding section but where the goods shown on this invoice are similar to those sold for home consumption, the fair market value exhibited thereon is not less than the aggregate of
    (a) the cost of production of the goods exported; and
    (b) an amount that is the same percentage of the cost of production of the goods exported as the gross profit on the similar goods is of the cost of production of the similar goods;
7. That the said fair market value is without
    (a) any discount or deduction not shown, allowed and deducted on invoices covering sales for home consumption in the country of export in the ordinary course of trade;
    (b) any deduction on account of any subsidy or drawback of Customs duty that has been allowed by the Government of any other country, or on account of any so-called royalty, rent or charge for use of any machine or goods of any description, that the seller or proprietor does or would usually charge thereon when the same are sold or leased or rented for use in the country of export; or
    (c) any discount or deduction on account of the amount of consideration or money value of any special arrangement between any persons interested therein, because of the exportation or intended exportation of such goods, or the right to territorial limits for the sale or use thereof;
8. That if the fair market value of the said goods described in this invoice is other than the value thereof as above specified, such fair market value has, to the best of my knowledge and belief, been fixed and determined under the authority of the Customs Act at the value exhibited in this invoice;
9. That no different invoice of the goods mentioned in the said invoice has been or will be furnished to any one by me or on my behalf;
10. That no arrangement or understanding affecting the purchase price of the said goods has been or will be made or entered into between the said exporter and purchaser or by any one on behalf of either of them other than as shown on the said invoice, either by way of discount, rebate, salary, compensation or in any other manner whatsoever;

(A)   That each article on this invoice is bona fide the produce or manufacture of the country specified on the invoice as its Country of Origin;
That each manufactured article on the invoice is in its present form ready for export to Canada has been finished in such specified country of origin, and not less than one-half the cost of production of

each such article has been produced through the industry of (Insert here name of country or countries)...............................
entitled to the benefits of treaty or convention rates or the British Preferential Tariff.

Dated at...

this...........................day of.....................19.... } (Signature)...............................
(Original copy must be signed in ink)

Note.—When invoicing goods which have been finished in a country specified on the invoice as its country of origin from materials originating in a country or countries entitled to the benefits of the Most Favoured Nation Tariff or the British Preferential Tariff, the names of the countries contributing to one-half the cost of production should be shown in the space provided in the certificate.

In the calculation of the cost of production for the purpose of determining the qualification for entry under the Most Favoured Nation Tariff none of the following items are to be included or considered, viz:—
1. Outside packages and expense of packing thereinto.   4. Customs or excise duty or tax paid or payable on imported materials.
2. Manufacturer's or exporter's profit or the profit or remuneration of any trader, broker, or other   5. Carriage, insurance, etc., from place of production or manufacture to port of shipment.
person dealing in the article in its finished mercantile condition.   6. Any other charges incurred or to be incurred subsequent to the completion of the manufac-
3. Royalties.   ture of the goods.
In cases where the vendor does not reside in the country of export or for other reasons the vendor is unable to sign the certificate both as to value and origin, a separate certificate of origin in prescribed form signed by the exporter in the country of export, bearing a full description of the goods and the marks and numbers of the packages, so that it may be identified with the shipment, will be accepted.

20. A M-A commercial invoice for shipments to Canada of $100 or more.

PACKING

Proper packing is very important. You'd be amazed at the rough treatment cartons usually get in shipping. There's no point in putting together a perfect order only to have it damaged in shipment because of faulty packing.

For packing materials you'll need strong corrugated cartons, heavy gummed tape, address labels, and stuffing material such as old newspapers.

Cartons. We used to get free cartons around town, the best source being liquor stores. If you don't do much shipping and use various sized cartons, you can investigate around town to find them. However, we now purchase boxes in three sizes from a local paper company. They cost from 23¢ to 56¢ a box, depending upon size. Since they're folded up and don't take up much room, we always have the size and number of boxes needed for a particular order. To find a local box supplier, look under "Paper Supplies" in the Yellow Pages. Big carton manufacturing companies will usually only take large orders (over 1,000) for a particular size box. We're not at that stage yet.

One thing to consider about cartons — the more beat up a carton is when you use it, the more tape you'll have to use to hold it together. With a new box, less tape is needed.

Stuffing. For stuffing material, we use old newspapers. When we run out, we can always find a neighbor with a cellar full of papers they're glad to get rid of. You can purchase packing materials such as tissue paper, and Styrofoam pieces, but this, of course, will increase your packing expenses.

To insure against damage you'll have to figure out the best way to pack your product. With breakable items it's important to have plenty of stuffing material around each piece. You might want to pack small items such as jewelry in a separate box, then in a larger box for better protection. Also consider inner and outer boxes if you ship glass and pottery. Each craft will lend itself to a particular packing method. We find, for instance, that if we neatly roll and stack our belts, they'll arrive at their destination in good shape. If we simply stuffed them into a box, they'd arrive bent and stretched. Try experimenting with different methods of packing your craft items.

No matter what your craft is, make sure the items inside the carton don't have room to rattle around. Stuff firmly, but don't overfill the carton so it bulges.

Tape. We suggest you use gummed tape at least 2½" wide. Reinforced gummed tape is even stronger, but it costs more. We used nonreinforced tape, but found it wasn't strong enough unless we doubled or tripled it. Now we use 3" reinforced tape and find that a little goes a long way. You can also get a tape dispenser that will simplify wetting and cutting the tape. Of the various models on the market we're not happy with our lower-priced dispenser, so you might consider investing in a good one.

Be sure to tape the carton securely. Here's a trick to help you put the first piece of tape on: stick it half on one side of the carton top only and then fold down the other sides; now press the top down (see Figure 21). Tape horizontally and vertically on both the top and bottom of the box. Always turn the box upside down to see if the bottom has enough tape on it. In general, the heavier the merchandise, the better you should pack it — that is, with stronger or more tape.

Labels. An address label isn't necessary because you can print the address right on the box. However, since a label stands out better, the shipper can pinpoint where the carton is going. Labels also look more professional, especially printed with your return address.

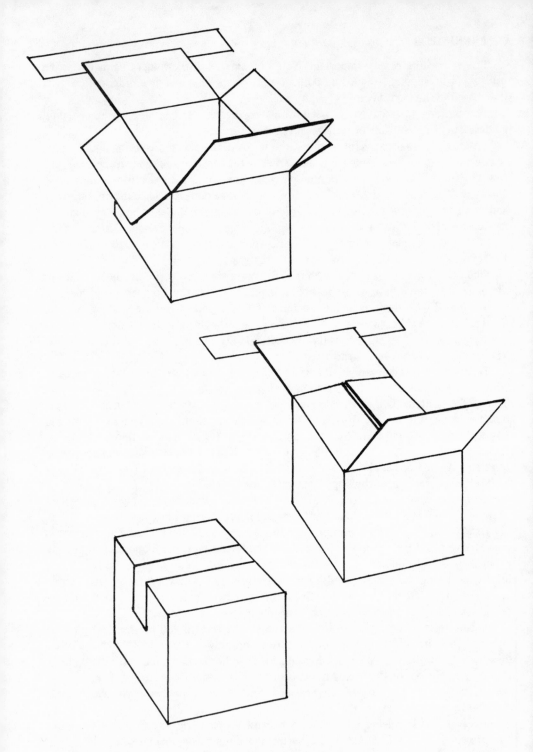

21. *Here's a simple way of putting your first piece of tape on the carton. This method allows you to get all four sides down tightly and evenly.*

A cheaper method is to purchase standard ones (see Figure 22) and use a rubber stamp for the return address. Labels and gummed tape can be purchased in a stationery or office-supply store.

Weighing the Package. We use a simple bathroom scale for weighing packages. For both parcel post and UPS, all weights are averaged to the next pound. For example, if the package weighs 3.5 pounds, call it 4 pounds. Anything under 8 ounces should be shipped third class if you want it to go the cheapest way.

Some large boxes are difficult to get on the scale while still being able to see how much they weigh. For these, we pick up the box, weigh ourselves holding the box, then subtract our own weight to figure out what the box weighs.

For parcel post shipments the post office will weigh the boxes for you and figure out the costs. For UPS, you must weigh the box and write the weight on the carton in front of your shipper's number (see Figure 23). You'll get a rubber stamp with your number on it when you sign the contract. If you don't have a contract or shipper's number with UPS, you'll still have to write the weight on the box. Just make sure it's clear.

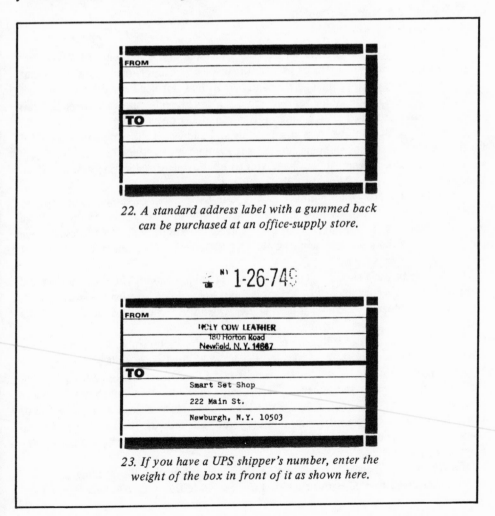

22. A standard address label with a gummed back can be purchased at an office-supply store.

23. If you have a UPS shipper's number, enter the weight of the box in front of it as shown here.

INVOICES/PACKING LISTS

Two forms commonly used in craft businesses are the invoice and packing list. An invoice is used to bill your customer for goods sent to him. A packing list shows all the items being shipped and should go with the package so the customer can check and see if all items were actually received. The invoice and packing list should match (see Figures 24 and 25).

Invoices. You can purchase invoice sets with carbons so both forms can be typed at once. You need at least three copies — the original for the customer, the second copy for your records, and the third copy to be used as a packing list. You can probably order them from your local office-supply store. If you can't find what you want, write to the following places and ask for their catalog of business forms:

Watts Business Forms, Inc.
Division of Lewis Business Forms, Inc.
Dillsburg, Pennsylvania 17019

New England Business Service, Inc.
Townsend, Massachusetts 01469

We type our invoices as soon as orders are received and put them in a "To Ship" folder. When an order is ready to be packed, the invoice is ready. Notice in Figure 24 that the invoice number is in the upper right-hand corner. Each invoice has a different number for reference in the future. Some forms come with printed, consecutive numbers. Get this kind if you can — it's easier than typing a different number on each one.

In the box after "To" we type in the name and address of the company to be billed for the merchandise. If the shipping address is the same, type in "same" under "Ship To." However, sometimes a company will ask you to bill one place and ship to another. If so, the place you ship to goes here.

Under "Customer's Order Number" we type in the number of the customer's order. "Shipping Date" is left blank until the order is actually shipped. Under "Ship Via," we put either parcel post, UPS, or the name of the trucking company. Under "Salesman" we put the name of the sales representative who took the order. You can leave this blank if you do all your own selling.

Under "Quantity," we list the number of each item purchased. The style number and name of the article goes under "Description." For "Unit Price" we list the price of each article or by the dozen, whichever is used under "Quantity." Under "Amount" we list the total cost.

Bills of Lading. Bills of lading are required when shipping by truck. You can purchase them at an office-supply store — ask for "Domestic Motor Carrier Bills of Lading" (see Figure 26). Note that you must list the weight and a description of the articles shipped. Different types of merchandise have different rates so the trucking company must know what you're shipping in order to figure out the charges. Make at least an original bill of lading for the trucking company and one copy for your records. It's also a good idea to make a copy for your customer and send it with the invoice so he can check on any delay from his end.

Packing Lists. When you finish typing the invoice, pull out the packing list copy. Some forms come printed with "Packing List" and have the price columns blanked out

Holy Cow Leather

180 HORTON ROAD
NEWFIELD, N.Y. 14867
TEL. 607-564-9022

Invoice No. _345_

TO ⌐ Smart Set Shop
222 Main St.
Newburgh, N.Y. 10503 ⌐

SHIP TO ⌐ Same ⌐

CUST'S ORDER NO.	SHIPPING DATE	SHIP VIA		SALESMAN	TERMS
A4223	11/23/73	UPS		Smith	1% 10 net 30

QUANTITY	DESCRIPTION	UNIT PRICE	AMOUNT
2dz	1 3/4" belts, assorted	50.00	100.00
1dz	3/4" belts, assorted	30.00	30.00
			$130.00
	UPS		1.03
			$131.03

WILCO BUSINESS FORMS, INC., ITHACA, N.Y. S/F NO. 100

24. This is an invoice form filled in with the information from the customer's order.

TO	Smart Set Shop 222 Main St. Newburgh, N.Y. 10503	SHIP TO	Same	

CUST'S ORDER NO. A4223	SHIPPING DATE	SHIP VIA UPS		SALESMAN Smith	TERMS 1% 10 net 30

QUANTITY	DESCRIPTION	UNIT PRICE	AMOUNT
2dz	1 3/4" belts, assorted	50.00	100.00
1dz	3/4" belts, assorted	30.00	30.00
			$130.00
	PACKING LIST		

WILCO BUSINESS FORMS, INC., ITHACA, N.Y. S/F NO. 100

25. *A regular invoice form can serve as a packing list, although some forms have the price columns blacked out.*

UNIFORM STRAIGHT BILL OF LADING   **Original—Not Negotiable—Domestic**

Shipper's No.

	Carrier	Agent's No.

RECEIVED, subject to the classifications and tariffs in effect on the date of the issue of this Bill of Lading,

From **HOLY COW LEATHER**   Date **November 23**   19 **73**

at **180 Horton Rd., Newfield, N.Y. 14867**

the property described below, in apparent good order, except as noted (contents and condition of contents of packages unknown), marked, consigned and destined as shown below, which said company (the word company being understood throughout this contract as meaning any person or corporation in possession of the property under this contract) agrees to carry to its usual place of delivery at said destination, if on its own railroad, water line, highway route or routes, or within the territory of its highway operations, otherwise to deliver to another carrier on the route to said destination. It is mutually agreed, as to each carrier of all or any of said property over all or any portion of said route to destination, and as to each party at any time interested in all or any of said property, that every service to be performed hereunder shall be subject to all the conditions not prohibited by law, whether printed or written, herein contained, including the conditions on back hereof, which are hereby agreed to by the shipper and accepted for himself and his assigns.

Consigned to **Smart Set Shop**

Destination **222 Main St.** ____Street **Newburgh** City **Belmont** County **New York** State

Routing

Delivering Carrier _____ Vehicle or Car Initial _____ No.

Collect On Delivery

$_____and remit to:_____

				C. O. D. charge to be paid by { Shipper ☐ / Consignee ☐ }
	Street	City	State	Subject to Section 7 of conditions, if this shipment is to be delivered to the consignee without recourse on the consignor, the consignor shall sign the following statement:

No. Packages	Description of Articles, Special Marks, and Exceptions	*Weight (Sub. to Cor.)	Class or Rate	Check Column	
6	leather handbags	140 lb.			The carrier shall not make delivery of this shipment without payment of freight and all other lawful charges.
					(Signature of Consignor)
					If charges are to be prepaid, write or stamp here, "To be Prepaid."
					Received $_____ to apply to prepayment of the charges on the property described hereon.
					Agent or Cashier
					Per _____ (The signature here acknowledges only the amount prepaid.)
					Charges Advanced:

*If the shipment moves between two ports by a carrier by water, the law requires that the bill of lading shall state whether it is "carrier's or shipper's weight."

NOTE — Where the rate is dependent on value shippers are required to state specifically in writing the agreed or declared value of the property. The agreed or declared value of the property is hereby specifically stated by the shipper to be not exceeding

_____ per _____

$

Holy Cow Leather ____ Shipper, Per _X. Taitslag_ _____ Agent, Per_____

Permanent post-office address of shipper,

6A 683 Redifprm

26. This bill of lading is necessary when shipping by truck.

because you only need the quantities of merchandise being shipped, not the prices. When the person at the receiving end gets the shipment and opens the carton, he checks to see that everything on the packing list is really in the box. Later on, the packing list is matched with the invoice for payment.

We used to stuff the packing list in the box just before sealing, so the person opening the box would see it right away. This worked fine, except for the times when we'd forget to enclose the packing list before sealing the box. Then it was a pain in the neck to open it again. Now we use plastic envelopes that stick to the outside of the box and say "Packing List Enclosed." This is a simpler method, and it makes certain the customer will see the packing list, not cut it in half while opening the carton (see Figure 27). You can order these envelopes from Watts Business Forms, Inc.

BILLING THE CUSTOMER

After the order is shipped, we type on the invoice the shipping date, the cost of shipping, and the total. Now it's ready to send to the customer (see Figure 28). We send the original to the customer and attach our copy to the order, job form, and bill of lading (if any).

27. *When the backing is removed, this plastic packing list envelope sticks to the front of the carton.*

Holy Cow Leather

180 HORTON ROAD
NEWFIELD, N.Y. 14867
TEL. 607-564-9022

Invoice No. _345_

TO	Smart Set Shop 222 Main St. Newburgh, N.Y. 10503	SHIP TO	Same		

CUST'S ORDER NO. A4223	SHIPPING DATE 11/23/73	SHIP VIA UPS		SALESMAN Smith	TERMS 1% 10 net 30

QUANTITY	DESCRIPTION	UNIT PRICE	AMOUNT
2dz	1 3/4" belts, assorted	50.00	100.00
1dz	3/4" belts, assorted	30.00	30.00
			$130.00
	UPS		1.03
			$131.03

WILCO BUSINESS FORMS, INC., ITHACA, N.Y. S/F NO. 100

28. This completed invoice with date of shipment and UPS charges is now ready to be sent to the customer.

The invoice should be mailed to the customer no later than a day or two after the merchandise is shipped. Customers prefer to receive the invoice before the shipment comes so they can expect its arrival, be aware of delays in shipment, and make arrangements for payment. Along with payment, the customer may send a copy of the invoice, the packing list, his own form, or just a check. In any case, you should keep your invoice copies in order (by date) in a handy "Accounts Receivable" folder so you can match all checks to invoice copies when they come in.

Terms. This refers to the terms of payment agreed on with the customer. "Net 30 days," a fairly standard term, means the customer must pay the invoice within 30 days from the date the order was shipped. You may want to offer a discount to customers who pay quickly. For instance, "1% 10 days net 30" means the customer may deduct 1% if he pays within 10 days. Otherwise, he must pay in full within 30 days. Department and chain stores often demand "3% 10 EOM" terms, meaning they can deduct 3% from the invoice, and the amount won't be due until the 10th of the following month. For example, if $100 worth of merchandise was shipped January 3, the customer would pay $97 on February 10th.

If you want payment right away, you can use terms of "net 10 days." Or if you want your money upon delivery, you can use C.O.D. terms, or "Cash On Delivery." If you're shipping parcel post, tell the postal clerk you want the package to go C.O.D. There will be an extra charge, but this can be collected from the customer. Keep in mind that parcel post only collects cash.

If you're shipping C.O.D. by UPS, you'll be provided with a special address label (see Figure 29) that is placed over your regular address label on the package. UPS will let the customer pay by check unless you specify cash or money order only. We mention this because in two cases we received a bad check for a C.O.D. shipment. However, if you're at the receiving end, you'll find it's difficult to keep large amounts of cash around for C.O.D. shipments. Make sure you add the additional C.O.D. charge to the total amount you want collected. In your UPS book, enter the C.O.D. amount also, as shown in Figure 30.

Who Pays Shipping Costs? Just as the terms of payment, the question of who'll pay shipping costs should be agreed upon initially by you and your customer. On orders or invoice forms you'll often see F.O.B., which means "Freight On Board." If your customer is in St. Louis and you're in Baltimore, "F.O.B. St. Louis" means you'll pay the shipping costs, and "F.O.B. Baltimore" means the customer will pay the shipping costs.

We never pay shipping costs on deliveries to our customers. It's standard procedure that the company ordering the merchandise pays to have it shipped. Some companies offer special deals where, if an order is prepaid or for a specified amount, the buyer won't have to pay shipping costs. We would suggest, however, that you state your terms as F.O.B. your factory.

If you ship by truck, the trucking company will collect the shipping charges for you on delivery or you can prepay them and bill your customer later. On parcel post and UPS you pay the costs in advance and add them to the total invoice amount.

SUMMING UP

Some of the forms and instructions, even for U.S. shipments, may seem complex when reading about them. But in practice, they really become quite routine. This book is

29. This tag provided by UPS for C.O.D. shipments should be affixed to the carton over the regular address label.

30. This page in a UPS book has a C.O.D. shipment. The amount is written in the C.O.D. column on the right.

meant for use by a business/craftsperson, and if you follow the steps one at a time, you'll save time and energy. Pretty soon, should you use United Parcel Service, you'll be looking forward to greeting the driver and enjoying a bit of conversation while you sign the book. Of course, when you get to be big business, you'll hire someone to do this and thereby miss out on a pleasant break. Such is the price of success.

CHECKLIST

1. Choose shipping method: parcel post, UPS, or truck.

2. Sign up with UPS for daily pick-up if UPS shipments are at least once a week.

3. Assemble packing materials: cartons, tape, stuffing, and labels.

4. Experiment and find the best method for packing your craft items.

5. Type invoice/packing list.

6. After packing, stuff thoroughly so merchandise is not loose in box.

7. Insert packing list before taping, or use outside envelopes.

8. Tape carton firmly on top and bottom.

9. Affix address label.

10. Stamp with UPS shipper stamp if you have one.

11. Weigh package.

12. Write weight on box.

13. Fill out bill of lading or UPS book. If C.O.D., fill out tag.

14. Finish filling out invoice and send to customer.

15. File your invoice copy in "Accounts Receivable" folder.

5

CREDIT AND COLLECTION

Once you've gone to the trouble of getting a sale, making the order, and packing and shipping it properly, you'll certainly want to be paid for your efforts. You might think that if you give someone a box of goods, it's only natural that they'll pay for them. However, you'll find that some will pay you three months late; others won't get around to it until prodded by reminders, and others may even go bankrupt. In any case, that's what this chapter is for – to explore the problems and procedures of collection in order to help you get back as close to 100% as possible.

DIRECT SALES

When you sell to neighbors, in a shop, or at a fair or fleamarket, you're selling direct, or retail. The general procedure is for the customer to pay you immediately for any purchases, and that eliminates a collection problem. One thing you'll have to watch out for, however, is bad checks.

You can take some precautions against bad checks by asking for identification such as a drivers license or credit card. Write the customer's drivers license number or credit card account number on the back of the check. If the license or card has a picture of the person, check to be sure it's the same person. Also, match signatures on the check and the identification.

If you decide it's safe to take checks only from your state or city, take telephone numbers also. The idea behind getting all this information is twofold – to discourage those who might write a bad check and to help you prosecute someone who does.

In two summers of accepting checks at fairs for our merchandise, we received only one bad check for $10.00. It came back from our bank marked "stop payment," which means the check writer deliberately stopped payment. If it had been marked "insufficient funds" it would mean there simply wasn't enough money in the account when the check went through. If you get a check back marked "insufficient funds," first try to get in touch with the person and tell him what happened. He may not have intentionally written a bad check, but was just short of funds at the time. Tell the person you will redeposit the check after a certain number of days. Then, simply deposit it again as you would a new check. However, if it comes back once more, the bank won't accept it a third time.

Since it's illegal to write bad checks, you can prosecute anyone who deliberately gives them out. If payment has been stopped, or the check comes back again after redepositing it for insufficient funds, take steps to prosecute. Contact the city prosecutor in the city where the bank printed on the check is located.

Don't wait too long to act. The person who deliberately writes bad checks probably writes many of them, moves often, and is difficult to locate. We feel it's important to prosecute even if the check is small. Why encourage someone to rip off others?

CONSIGNMENT

Refer to Chapter 9 for detailed information on consignment. Since you're giving a shop goods without payment, make sure you have them sign a contract. Then check periodically (more often initially) to see if they've made any sales. Keep accurate records and don't let them go for more than a month without paying you.

WHOLESALE

In wholesale selling, or selling in large quantities, you'll find good collection procedures very important. When taking an order from a store, you ship it in good faith and then sit back and wait for your money. Perhaps you gave terms of net 30 days (see Chapter 4), and therefore a month after shipping the order, you expect the check to arrive. What do you do if it never arrives? Should you have given this particular store terms of net 30 days in the first place? How do you maintain good relationships with your customers while being firm about receiving payments on time?

Credit Rating. Before you offer a store any terms at all, you should find out what its credit rating is. How long has it been in operation? What other suppliers offer it credit? How does the store pay them — promptly or slowly? Chances are that if this store pays everyone else promptly, has been in business for a number of years, and has a sizeable bank balance, it will probably also pay you promptly.

When you get an order from a new store, ask for the name of their bank and at least three references (names of suppliers they deal with regularly). Contact these references and ask what their experience has been with this particular store. Basically, you'll want to know how long they've sold to it, what the highest amount of credit given has been, and how prompt their payments are.

Credit Organizations. There are credit organizations who will do this checking for you. They get detailed information on businesses and compile it into reports that are offered to their members. If your business is all local, then use a local credit association. There's usually a set yearly fee that covers a certain number of reports, then an additional charge for reports over this number.

Dun & Bradstreet is the largest national credit organization. They give business credit ratings and then list these ratings in books. For example, a "2" rating means the company pays promptly, and a "4" rating indicates poor payments. You can subscribe to Dun & Bradstreet on a state or national basis. Besides the books, which are revised four times a year, they provide a certain number of detailed reports.

It will cost you money to join a local credit organization or subscribe to Dun & Bradstreet. Therefore, you have to try to estimate what they'll save you in the way of avoiding uncollectible debts and time previously spent checking out credit references. Have someone from several of these organizations come and talk to you about their services. Then examine your own situation to determine whether or not to use them.

C.O.D. and Terms. We discussed C.O.D., or "Cash on Delivery," in Chapter 4. If, after checking out a new store's credit rating, you decide they're too risky, tell them you'll only ship C.O.D.

Some stores prefer C.O.D. anyway, especially on small orders. However, there's a charge for shipping C.O.D. whether you ship by truck, parcel post, or UPS. Add this charge to the cost of the order along with shipping costs. Because of the extra cost and the inconvenience of having to pay on delivery, some stores won't accept C.O.D. shipments. So make sure this method of shipment is agreed on in advance.

When you ship C.O.D. via parcel post, the post office will accept only cash or money order for the goods. However, UPS or a trucker will accept a company check unless you specify otherwise. If you want to be perfectly safe, specify "cash," "certified check," or "money order only." But make sure you notify the store in advance so they can have it ready when the delivery arrives.

Various discount terms were also discussed in Chapter 4. These are terms that offer a discount to the customer for paying early, 2% 10, net 30, for example. The customer may pay the full price in 30 days, however, if he pays in 10 days, he's allowed to deduct 2% from the total amount. The reason for offering such terms is to encourage stores to pay early. However, you'll find that some will pay in 30 days or later, and still deduct the discount. The only way to avoid this is to print on your invoice, "No discount allowed after (date)."

When to Expect Payment. Some stores will always pay early, even if you don't offer a discount. If you offer a discount for payment within 10 days, some will write a check on exactly the 10th day from the date of shipment or date of receipt so you'll probably receive payment in about 15 days. Others will take the full 30 days and write their checks on exactly the 30th day from date of shipment. Even though these checks are on time, it will take you about 35 days to get them, allowing for mailing time. There are also those who figure that as long as they're within the vicinity of 30 days they're on time. These checks could dribble in from 35 to 60 days after shipment. Anything later than this needs some action.

Collection Procedures. When setting up a collection system you must follow it faithfully for it to be effective. First, decide at what point you feel payment is too late. You may want to wait a full 30 days after payment is due. (If an order is shipped on January 1st on 30 day terms, it's due February 1st. If you wait another 30 days, you'd start collection procedures on March 1st.) Or you may decide you can't wait that long and begin to take action 10 or 20 days after an invoice is past due.

Whatever you decide, on the date the invoice becomes past due, say 30 days, send out your first notice. There are several ways to do this. You could simply make a duplicate of the past-due invoice, write "reminder" at the top, and send it to the customer. Or you could write a letter as we've shown in Figure 31. It's important that the initial reminder be friendly, not threatening. You don't want to antagonize a good customer who might simply have overlooked payment.

Holy Cow Leather

180 HORTON ROAD
NEWFIELD, NEW YORK 14867

_____

PHONE: (607) 564 - 9022

January 3, 1974

The Smart Shop
Main Street
Maplewood, N.J. 00055

Gentlepeople:

We would like to call your attention to our Invoice #543
dated November 3rd, 1973 in the amount of $304.56. To date
we have not received payment for this invoice.

We would appreciate your attention to this matter as soon as
possible. If payment is in the mail, please disregard this
notice.

Thank you.

                              Sincerely,

                              HOLY COW LEATHER

                              Lyn Taetzsch

_31. This is an example of a letter you might send to an account whose invoice is 10 to 30
days past due._

The next step is to mark in your calendar when the second notice should be sent if payment still hasn't come in. Send the second notice 10 days after the first, so you don't wait around another month without payment. Your next letter should be more firm and insistent. Or you can purchase a rubber stamp that says "Second Notice" and stamp this on a copy of the invoice.

If you still don't receive payment within 10 days, send a final notice warning that if payment isn't received within 10 days, action will be taken. We'll discuss what action you can take later.

There's a collection expediter form you can purchase from Watts Business Forms (see p. 46 for address) that comes in a set of three notices (see Figure 32). You only have to type in the name of the customer, your name, the date of notice, due date, and amount due. It simplifies the collection procedure by eliminating letters, invoice copying, etc.

Collection Agencies. Usually, credit agencies also provide collection services. Dun & Bradstreet has a separate collection service available at a small yearly fee. The collection agency is the place you turn to when the store repeatedly ignores your notices. Ten days after you send your last notice, turn the account over to one of these agencies.

When the agency gets the account for collection, the standard procedure is to write an initial letter on their stationery. If the account pays within 10 days, you receive the whole amount without paying them anything. After that, they take a percentage of the amount past due, depending upon the amount of time and effort they spend in collection. They use telephone calls, letters, etc., to try to collect. Finally, if all else fails they'll use an attorney and possibly take the case to court. As you can well imagine, at this point a big chunk will be taken out of the total, and you'll end up with a fraction of the amount due.

This is why you should carefully check accounts *before* you give them credit. If you give credit to all stores without checking their credit, some will naturally be bad risks and end up costing you money. No matter how careful you are, however, you may occasionally end up with a bad one, and in these cases the collection agency will be very useful. It's better to collect part of a bad debt than none at all.

CHECKLIST

1. If you take checks for direct retail sales, ask for identification, write down phone numbers, license numbers, etc.

2. On consignment accounts, make sure they sign a contract, and check on them often, especially in the beginning.

3. Before offering a new store terms, check their credit rating. Check out at least three references and their bank.

4. Explore credit agencies, both local and national (Dun & Bradstreet, for example). Examine their services and decide if it will be profitable in the long run to subscribe to them.

5. If a store doesn't have a good credit rating, ship C.O.D. only. To be safe, insist on cash, certified check, or money order.

FRIENDLY REMINDER!

HOLY COW LEATHER
180 Horton Rd.
Newfield, N.Y. 14867

NO DOUBT YOU HAVE OVERLOOKED PAYMENT. YOUR
REMITTANCE BY RETURN MAIL WILL BE APPRECIATED.

DATE OF NOTICE	DUE DATE	AMOUNT DUE
1/2/74	12/2/74	$100.00

TO
Smiths Boutique Shop
Main Street
Anywhere, U.S.A.

THANK YOU

IF YOUR REMITTANCE HAS
ALREADY BEEN SENT, PLEASE
DISREGARD THIS NOTICE.

PAYMENT PAST DUE

HOLY COW LEATHER
180 Horton Rd.
Newfield, N.Y. 14867

WE SHALL APPRECIATE YOUR PROMPT
ATTENTION, AND A REMITTANCE.

DATE OF NOTICE	DUE DATE	AMOUNT DUE
1/12/74	12/2/74	$100.00

TO
Smiths Boutique Shop
Main Street
Anywhere, U.S.A.

THANK YOU

IF YOUR REMITTANCE HAS
ALREADY BEEN SENT, PLEASE
DISREGARD THIS NOTICE.

DELINQUENT PAYMENT NOTICE

HOLY COW LEATHER
180 Horton Rd.
Newfield, N.Y. 14867

REPEATED REQUESTS FOR SETTLEMENT OF YOUR PAST
DUE ACCOUNT HAVE APPARENTLY BEEN IGNORED. UNLESS
PAYMENT IS RECEIVED WITHIN TEN DAYS, IMMEDIATE ACTION
TO COLLECT THIS PAYMENT WILL BE TAKEN.

DATE OF NOTICE	DUE DATE	AMOUNT DUE
1/22/74	12/2/74	$100.00

TO
Smiths Boutique Shop
Main Street
Anywhere, U.S.A.

THANK YOU

---

32. Collection expediter forms come in a set of three copies. Note how each subsequent notice gets stronger, and that each is dated 10 days from the previous notice.

6. If a store has a good credit rating, offer them terms such as net 30 days, or 2% 10 net 30.

7. Decide on a past due limit for beginning collection procedures, such as 10, 20, or 30 days. Don't delay more than 30 days.

8. At the end of your past due limit, begin collection procedure with an initial letter, reminder, or notice. Mark your calendar for attention in 10 days.

9. Every 10 days, send the next notice if an account has still not paid.

10. After final notice, wait 10 days for collection, then send the account to a collection agency.

PAPERWORK
AND RECORDS

This end of your business may seem the least important and very unappealing. But keeping good records and filing systems, you'll be able to run your business more efficiently. You'll know what's going on at all times, and at the end of the year you'll have the necessary information for analysis and tax forms. So don't put off setting up bookkeeping and filing systems because in the long run they'll be worth the extra work.

SIMPLE BOOKKEEPING SYSTEM

The system we used when first starting out was simply a monthly recording of every business dollar spent and taken in (see Figure 33). Every time money was spent, the date, amount, and purpose were recorded in the left-hand columns. Every time money was received (earned), the date, description, and amount were recorded on the right-hand side.

In any system it's important to make sure everything is recorded. Save all bills, receipts, etc., even for small amounts. When buying postage stamps for your business, ask the clerk for a receipt. If items on your shopping list are for your business, circle them and keep the receipt. If you pay cash and don't get a receipt, be sure to make a note. Each day enter these items in your book, or save them and do it once a week.

Profit or Loss. At the end of the month after all monies in and out are recorded, total both columns. If the "Money In" column is greater than the "Money Out," you made a profit that month. If the "Money Out" is greater, you show a loss.

However, problems arise when you purchase supplies in one month that aren't used up until the next month, or even later. Also, if you sell on credit, you won't collect your money for a month or two. Therefore, your monthly profit and loss figure won't be an accurate indication of how your business is doing. We recommend this simple system only if your business is small and you only accept cash, not credit.

	Out			In	
Date	Item	Amount	Date	Item	Amount
9/2	rent	$100.00	9/1	Sumerson Fair	$325.00
9/4	leather	250.00	9/2	consignment	75.00
9/5	alcohol	.75	9/4	refund – Tandy	1.50

33. This page in a simple "In and Out" bookkeeping system lists all expenditures and income for September.

DOUBLE-ENTRY SYSTEM

To set up a really sophisticated double-entry bookkeeping system, it's advisable to call in an accountant. However, we've devised a modified system that's easy to keep, provides the necessary information and records, and is molded for a craft business.

"Double-entry" simply means that you make a double entry for every amount you spend or receive. In other words, each transaction is recorded twice. For example, if you spend $10.00 for a tool, you'd enter it in two places — as a debit under "Tools," and a credit under "Cash." Don't let the terms "debit" and "credit" confuse you. Double-entry bookkeeping systems are set in "T-accounts," with the left side of the "T" labeled "Debit" and the right side "Credit." "Debit" equals left, "credit" equals right. That's all there is to it.

The sample T-accounts in Figure 34 illustrate two transactions. In the first, a telephone bill of $20.43 was paid on 5/11. On the Utilities T-account, "5/11" is entered under "Date," "telephone" under "Item," and "$20.43" under "Debit." Now to make our double entry, we must enter this $20.43 on the credit side of another T-account. By listing the $20.43 under the credit column of the Cash T-account, we've balanced out our entry.

The principle behind entering everything twice is this: if you spend $40.00 on a set of tools for your business, you've depleted your cash resources. But you've also increased the business' resources; in particular, its tools. In Chapter 7 you'll see how these transactions balance out in assets and liabilities.

The second transaction in Figure 34 is a payment of an electric and gas bill. Note that it's recorded under "Debit" on the Utilities T-account and under "Credit" on the Cash T-account. The important thing is to be consistent. If an item is entered on the debit side of one account, it must be entered on the credit side of another account. Since money spent by the business is listed on the credit side of the Cash T-account, on which side would you record money received? On the debit side, naturally. About as natural as scratching your neck with your foot, but don't let it throw you. A little practice will make it easier, and it's an invaluable tool for figuring taxes.

Setting Up T-accounts. One T-account you'll definitely need is a Cash account. On this page you record everything that comes in under "Debit," and everything you spend under "Credit" (see Figure 35). Note that the debit side lists all the checks recieved from stores, refunds, cash sales, etc. The credit side lists all checks for supplies and services, and cash used for expenses, etc. Money listed in the Cash account should include deposits in all business checking accounts and savings accounts, as well as uncashed checks and money on hand.

The opposite of Cash credit listings are cost accounts — for each item listed under Cash credit there must be an account where you list it as a debit. Some cost accounts you might find useful are: Payroll, Expenses, Advertising, Tools & Equipment, Basic Materials (leather, clay, glass, etc.), Utilities, Rent, Sales Commissions, Freight, and Office Supplies. Basically, you'll need to cover every major area in which you spend money. Then for odd expenditures, set up a Miscellaneous Expenses account.

The opposite of cash debit listings are receivables. You'll need one or more account headings for these. If all your selling is done wholesale on a credit basis, all you'll need is an Accounts Receivable account to cover them. Every time you receive a check from a customer, record it on the credit side of your Accounts Receivable account and the debit side of your Cash account (see Figure 36).

Cash

Date	Item	Debit	Date	Item	Credit
			5/11	telephone –May	$20.43
			5/12	elec. & gas	15.25

Utilities

Date	Item	Debit	Date	Item	Credit
5/11	telephone –May	$20.43			
5/12	elec. & gas	15.25			

34 Two typical transactions are shown in this Utilities T-account and Cash T-account.

Cash

Date	Item	Debit	Date	Item	Credit
5/1	Smart Shop	$105.50	5/1	rent	$100.00
5/2	Bons Dress	200.00	5/3	Bennies Buckles	85.68
5/3	Tandy-refund	.75	5/8	sales commissions	76.42
5/6	The Love Shop	95.43	5/9	Berman Leather	205.53
	cash sale	10.05			
5/7	Northill Craft Fair	213.00			

35. *In this Cash T-account note that the debit side lists monies in and the credit side lists monies out.*

Accounts Receivable

Date	Item	Debit	Date	Item	Credit
			5/2	Bubbles Boutique	$105.50
			5/3	Sharp Shop	250.00
			5/6	Bons Dress	85.00

Cash

Date	Item	Debit	Date	Item	Credit
5/2	Bubbles Boutique	$105.50			
5/3	Sharp Shop	250.00			
5/6	Bons Dress	85.00			

36. *When you receive a check from an account, record it on the credit side of Accounts Receivable and on the debit side of Cash.*

If you also receive money from consignment and cash sales, you'll need another page to cover these items. You could lump them together and call it "Cash Sales, Consignment & Fairs," or you could set up a separate page for each. The important thing is to record money received from these items on the credit side of an account, since they'll be recorded on the debit side of Cash.

Accounts Receivable Debits. We previously stated that you should list checks received for wholesale sales under the credit side of Accounts Receivable account. The debit side of this account is used to record shipments. Every time you ship an order to a customer, list the date of shipment, the customer's name, and the amount of the invoice on the debit side.

Since every entry must be recorded in two places, you now need to record shipments in a credit column. Set up an account called "Shipments" and list each one on the credit side (see Figure 37).

Returns and Refunds. In general, your Shipments account will have only the credit columns filled in. But if you should have a customer refuse an order or return it for some reason, this would be recorded in the debit column (in Figure 38, note that it's recorded in the debit column of Shipments and the credit column of Accounts Receivable).

Accounts Receivable

Date	Item	Debit	Date	Item	Credit
5/2	Tally-Ho Shop	$305.00			
5/4	The Fling Shop	100.00			
5/5	Craft Cellar	83.00			

Shipments

Date	Item	Debit	Date	Item	Credit
			5/2	Tally-Ho Shop	$305.00
			5/4	The Fling Shop	100.00
			5/5	Craft Cellar	83.00

37. When you ship an order, record it on the credit side of Shipments and the debit side of Accounts Receivable, as illustrated here.

A refund from one of your suppliers would be cash in and is recorded on the debit side of your Cash account. It should also be recorded on the credit side of the corresponding cost account (see Figure 39).

Balance Columns. It's a good idea to add a balance column to the right of each account page. By keeping a running balance, you'll be able to tell at a glance how much cash you have on hand, how much money people owe you, and what you've spent to date on each payable page.

On the Cash account, your balance is figured by subtracting the credit amounts from the debit amounts. If your Cash account ever shows a minus balance, and it's not simply a bookkeeping error, then your checking account must be overdrawn (see Figure 40 for an illustration of a Cash account with a balance column).

On all cost accounts such as Utilities, and Rent, the balance is figured by adding the debits and subtracting the credits. The balance should show the total amount spent in that category to date. To separate monthly balances from yearly balances, you should have two balance columns. Figure 41 is an illustration of a Basic Materials account with the monthly and cumulative columns filled in. Notice that the refund under credit is subtracted from the purchases, or debits.

Your Accounts Receivable balance column is very important. It shows at a glance how much money your customers owe you. This balance is figured by subtracting the credits from the debits. In Figure 42 a balanced Accounts Receivable account, we see that $8,400 worth of goods has been shipped to customers and is still not paid for.

Money Taken Out of the Business. When you or your partners take money out of the business for your personal use, it's recorded in a Draw account. Suppose there are two partners in the business, Bob and Bill. The business is doing well enough so that each can take out of it $200.00 per month. Set up one page as "Bob's Draw," and another as "Bill's Draw." When each partner takes his money it should be listed as a debit in his Draw account and a credit in the Cash account.

In Figure 43 are entries of Bob's Draw, Bill's Draw, and the Cash account, showing withdrawal of money from the business. On February 1st each partner took $200.00. This is entered in the debit column of each partner's Draw and the credit column of the Cash account. On March 1st each partner took another $200.00, which is similarly recorded. Notice that the balance for each partner is now $400.00.

INDEX CARD FILE

A 3" X 5" card file box with index cards and alphabetical separators is a handy item to keep near your telephone for quick reference. On the cards keep names, addresses, and telephone numbers that are frequently used: suppliers, sales representatives, employees, the post office, and printers.

Write as much information as possible on these cards. For example, if you deal with a printer on a regular basis, jot down standard prices on letterhead, or envelopes as well as the name of the person you usually deal with. If someone is only in during certain hours, write this down also.

We also keep a card under the name of our store listing our New York State resale number and Dun & Bradstreet number. This helps us to find these numbers quickly when writing or calling in orders to suppliers. Another handy card lists the 3rd and 4th class postal rates.

Accounts Receivable

Date	Item	Debit	Date	Item	Credit
			5/2	Tally-Ho Shop-ref.	$305.00

Shipments

Date	Item	Debit	Date	Item	Credit
5/2	Tally-Ho Shop-ref.	$305.00			

38. Here is how to record a refused shipment. Note that it is listed on the debit side of Shipments and the credit side of Accounts Receivable.

Tools

Date	Item	Debit	Date	Item	Credit
			5/14	refund- Tandy	$1.05

Cash

Date	Item	Debit	Date	Item	Credit
5/14	refund- Tandy	$1.05			

39. When you receive a refund from a supplier, list the amount on the debit side of Cash and the credit side of the corresponding cost account, as in this Tools T-account.

Cash

Date	Item	Debit	Date	Item	Credit	Bal.
5/11	Bubbles Boutique	$200.00	5/16	laces	$ 25.00	$ 505.00
	Hot Shops	750.00	5/18	Tandy-tools	34.00	
				telephone	43.00	$1,365.00
5/13	refund-dye	12.00	5/21	leather	500.00	
5/20	Craft Fair	250.00	5/22	postage	4.35	
5/25	Sun Shop	342.00	5/26	elec. & gas	15.00	
			5/30	sales commissions	150.00	$1,287.65

40. By adding a balance column to your Cash account, you can keep up-to-date on your cash balance. Note how the credits have been subtracted from the debits to arrive at the balance.

Basic Materials

Date	Item	Debit	Date	Item	Credit	Mo.Bal.	Cum.Bal
5/2	leather	$500.00				$500.00	$500.00
5/4	buckles	50.00				550.00	550.00
5/16	laces	25.00				575.00	575.00
			5/18	refund-leather	$3.50	571.50	571.50
5/25	leather	200.00				771.50	771.50
6/2	buckles	75.00				75.00	846.50
6/6	keyrings	20.00				95.00	866.50

41. This is a Basic Materials account with monthly and cumulative balance columns.

Accounts Receivable

Date	Item	Debit	Date	Item	Credit	Bal.
5/2	Bubbles Boutique	$ 200.00	5/6	Shoe Shop	$ 100.00	
	Jumpin' Jack	500.00	5/7	Find It Here	340.00	
5/3	Up Shop	350.00	5/8	Sew & Show	50.00	
5/4	Bess Dress	200.00	5/9	Fun Shop	125.00	$9,365.00
	Shoe Stop	850.00				
	Leather Hide-Out	1,000.00				
5/5	Hot Shop	750.00				
	Right On	600.00				
5/7	Crafts Corner	1,250.00				
	Fun Fair	380.00				
5/8	Great Gifts	1,480.00				
5/9	Show Shine	2,420.00				$9,365.00
5/11	Flowers n Things	250.00	5/11	Bubbles Boutique	200.00	
	Hand Mades	425.00		Hot Shop	750.00	
5/12	Quick Find	1,340.00	5/14	Fun Fair	380.00	
5/14	Show's On	825.00	5/15	Right On	600.00	
5/15	Sun Shop	342.00		Crafts Corner	1,250.00	
	Swap Shop	58.00	5/16	Rock Shop	1,345.00	
5/16	Belts More	320.00				$8,400.00

42. By keeping a balance column on your Accounts Receivable account you'll always know how much money is owed to you.

Bob's Draw

Date	Item	Debit	Date	Item	Credit	Bal.
2/1	check #350	$200.00				$200.00
3/1	check #374	200.00				400.00

Bill's Draw

Date	Item	Debit	Date	Item	Credit	Bal.
2/1	check #351	$200.00				$200.00
3/1	check #375	200.00				400.00

Cash

Date	Item	Debit	Date	Item	Credit	Bal.
			2/1	Bob's draw	$200.00	
				Bill's draw	200.00	
			3/1	Bob's draw	200.00	
				Bill's draw	200.00	

43. This shows the Draw accounts of two partners and how these draws are recorded in the Cash account.

A STANDARD USED FILE CABINET

You can probably pick up used 8½" X 11" file cabinets rather cheaply by looking in your daily newspaper under "Items For Sale." You can often get them at end-of-the-year school sales, from companies going out of business, or if you want a new one, at an office equipment store.

Along with the file cabinet, you'll need a box of 8½" X 11" manilla folders. They come in various "cuts" or tabs — the standard tab is 1/3 cut, but 1/4 or 1/5 will do. You can buy gummed labels for the folders, or you can simply print the heading right on the folder tab.

Folder Headings. You'll need a folder for every area in which there are things to file. For instance, if your correspondence is very light, mark a folder "Correspondence" for all letters received and copies of letters sent (make certain you keep a copy of every business letter sent out). If you find that you correspond heavily with certain people or companies, make separate folders for them.

We have a general correspondence folder, but we keep separate folders for each of our sales representatives. In these folders we keep everything that pertains to these reps — correspondence, copies of commission statements, sample invoices, etc. Other general folders you might want to make are: Expenses, Advertising, Printing, Bank Statements, Business Papers, Employee's Time Sheets, and Form Letters.

Payables. When we first set up our filing system, we had one folder marked "Expenditures" into which we put every paid bill, sales receipt, etc., for everything we bought for the business. We've since learned that it's much more useful to have a separate folder for each major company we do business with. For example, we have a folder for the company we buy buckles from, and one for each company we buy leather from.

If you don't want to break it down this far, at least have a folder for each cost account in your books, such as Utilities, Basic Supplies, Freight, and Office Supplies. The reason we suggest this breakdown is that we've spent a lot of time pouring through the whole Expenditures folder looking for an old invoice to find the price of a certain buckle. An Expenditures folder may seem thin and manageable at first, but it soon becomes a bulky mess.

Receivables. In the past, when a customer paid our invoice (see Chapter 4), we took a copy out of the Accounts Receivable folder, marked it "Paid (date)," and filed it in a folder called "Completed Sales." This is another folder that started out thin and in a few months was overflowing. Often we wanted to find out what a customer ordered, or how quickly they paid their last invoice. Again, we had to pour through the entire folder.

Now we have a folder for each customer, and we file copies of paid invoices, correspondence, copies of Dun & Bradstreet reports, etc. So whenever we want to know something about a customer, we simply look in their folder. You may feel this uses up too many folders, especially if you have a lot of customers, but you'll find it worth the trouble in the long run.

ACCOUNTS RECEIVABLE CARD FILE

Another item we've added to our system is an Accounts Receivable card file. We make up a 5" X 8" index card for each customer and record on it all shipments and payments by date (see Figure 44). Note that the name and address of the company is in

The Shoe Shop
110 MAIN ST.
ANYWHERE, U.S.A.   (Rep: SMITH)

			DR	CR	BAL
2	1	Shipment	300 00		300 00
2	10	Payment (\$6 Discount)		300 00	
3	15	Shipment	250 00		250 00
3	20	Shipment	80 00		330 00
3	22	Payment (\$5 Discount)		250 00	80 00
3	29	Payment (1.60 Discount)		80 00	

44. *This 5" x 8" Receivables card shows several shipments and payments by the customer.*

the upper left-hand corner. In the upper right-hand corner we pencil in their current credit rating (these ratings change — thus the pencil). In parentheses on the top line we list the sales representative, if any.

Note the columns for debit (Dr.), credit (Cr.) and balance (Bal.). You can see from the transactions listed on this sample card that this account always pays its bills early and takes the discount. However, you can't always tell how an account will pay by its credit rating. Some will have excellent ratings on paying others, but they'll pay slowly. By keeping these cards up-to-date on each customer, you can tell at a glance what their payment record is, how much is past due, and whether or not to extend more credit.

SUMMING UP

The bookkeeping and filing procedures described in this chapter may have seemed complicated and tedious to you. However, once you've spent the initial time setting them up, they'll require an afternoon a week or so to keep up-to-date. They'll provide you with useful information, and in the long run, save you time and effort.

CHECKLIST

1. Decide on either the "Simple In-and-Out" or "Double-Entry" system.

2. If you use the simple system, set up your book by month with money spent in the left-hand column and money taken in the right-hand column.

3. If you use the double-entry system, set up each T-account with debit columns on the left, credit columns on the right, and balance columns on the extreme right.

4. Make an account for Cash, one for each major cost account, Accounts Receivable, Shipments, Fairs-Consignment-Direct Sales (if you have any), and Draw.

5. Money spent for supplies and other payables is entered on the debit side of the cost account and the credit side of the Cash account.

6. Money received from customers, consignment, fairs, etc., goes on the credit side of these accounts, and the debit side of Cash.

7. Shipments are entered on the credit side of Shipments, and the debit side of Accounts Receivable.

8. Refunds are entered on the credit side of the payable account in which the refund was made, and the debit side of Cash.

9. Returns or refused shipments are entered on the debit side of Shipments, the credit side of Accounts Receivable.

10. When you or your partners take money out of the business, record the amount in the debit column of the Draw account and the credit column of Cash.

11. Set up a 3″ × 5″ card file with names, addresses, telephone numbers, etc., by the telephone. Examples: suppliers, sales representatives, employees, UPS, post office, trucking companies.

12. Set up an 8½″ × 11″ file cabinet. Make a folder for every area in which you'll have things to file, such as correspondence, expenses, taxes, and advertising.

13. We recommend a separate 8½″ × 11″ file folder for every major supplier, or each cost account.

14. We recommend a separate 8½″ × 11″ file folder for each customer in which you file paid invoices, credit information, and correspondence.

15. A 5″ × 8″ Accounts Receivable card file listing shipments and payments by date is also a very useful system.

7

ANALYZING
YOUR PROGRESS

As time progresses you'll want to know what kind of progress your craft business is making. Are you actually making a profit? Is the net value of your business increasing? What percentage do you spend on raw materials, advertising, labor, etc.?

An analysis of your progress will be especially important when you want to apply for a bank or small business association loan. It will also be important when you're filling out a credit association form on your business to get credit from your supplier. Finally, an analysis will be necessary when filling out your income tax reports. Keeping good records (as outlined in Chapter 6) is the first step toward analysis. In this chapter we'll show you how to utilize these records when making income statements, balance sheets, and other analyses.

ASSETS, LIABILITIES, AND EQUITY

The assets of a business are everything it owns of monetary value — cash, merchandise, tools, equipment, raw materials, buildings, and land. Assets also include money owed to the business for services performed or goods shipped. This means assets will include accounts receivable.

The liabilities of a business are its debts — goods bought on credit, salaries owed to employees, and loans owed to banks, etc. If the business owns a piece of property, the value of the property is an asset, but the remaining mortgage owed is a liability.

Equity is the interest of the owners of a business in the business assets. For example, if you start a new business with $3,000 from your savings, the business now has assets of $3,000 cash, no liabilities, and your owner equity, or capital, is $3,000. Equity is the difference between the assets and the liabilities.

Balance Sheet. A balance sheet showing the business's assets, liabilities, and owner equity should be made at least once a year. If you're applying for a loan or credit rating, make another balance sheet (unless your year-end report was within three months).

A simple example will illustrate the set-up of a balance sheet. Suppose you start your business on 12/1/73 with $5,000 savings and a bank loan for $5,000. You then buy $3,000 worth of raw materials and tools (see Figure 45). Note that the $7,000 cash plus the $3,000 in materials and tools give total assets of $10,000. The only liability is the $5,000 bank loan. Your owner's equity is therefore $5,000, which was your initial investment.

After six months of operation, your balance sheet may look like the one in Figure 46. The business has been in operation for six months, and it has built up an accounts receivable of $5,000. This means that on 5/1/74, $5,000 was owed to the business by customers for goods already shipped.

The inventory covers small tools and raw materials, plus goods partially finished. To compute the value of your inventory, it's necessary, of course, to take a physical inventory when making a balance sheet (see Chapter 3, Inventory Systems). This is done by counting all items in inventory, including raw materials, work in process, and finished goods. To compute the value of your inventory, multiply the quantity of each item times the cost. You can determine the value of the materials on hand at what they originally cost you or what you'll have to pay to replace them — as long as you consistently use the same method.

Suppose at the beginning of the year you paid $1,000 for an insurance policy on the business. After six months, $500 had been paid but not yet used. This is called "prepaid insurance."

Under liabilities, the accounts payable are bills you owe for merchandise and services that you've received but not paid for. The loan that should be listed here is the remainder of the $5,000 loan discussed above. $1,500 was paid off, leaving $3,500 still due.

To arrive at owner's equity first add the assets and then add the liabilities. When you subtract the liabilities from the assets, the owners equity is $10,000. Six months ago when the business started, it was only $5,000. Thus the business has grown by $5,000.

INCOME STATEMENT

An income, or operating statement, should be made at the end of every month. Its basic purpose is to show whether there was a profit or loss during a certain period of time. While a balance sheet shows the value of the business on a particular date, an income statement shows the profit or loss for a particular period of time. To find out whether a profit or loss was made, subtract the cost of making your products from the total amount of money received for them.

In Figure 47, an income statement for a one-month period, note that there was a net income of $1,000. The revenues total is arrived at by adding up all the money received for goods sold — wholesale, at craft fairs, and to neighbors, etc. Operating expenses include all the money spent to make these goods. Use the month-end totals from each of your payables accounts to arrive at these figures. After subtracting operating expenses from revenues, you have a net income of $1,000.

Income Statement Accuracy. However, there are several problems with the income statement we've just described. For example, you may have shipped $6,000 worth of goods that month. The $5,000 in revenues actually received reflects money paid for goods shipped in previous months. Therefore the $5,000 figure doesn't represent accurately what the business did. To get a more accurate revenue figure, list the total amount

Balance Sheet: 12/1/73

Assets		Liabilities	
Cash	$ 7,000	Loans	$ 5,000
Inventory	3,000		
	$10,000		
		Owner's Equity	$ 5,000
Total Assets	$10,000	Total Liab. & Owner's Equity	$10,000

45. *A simple balance sheet shows the assets and liabilities at the start of a business. The owner's equity, or initial investment, is $5,000.*

Balance Sheet: 5/1/74

Assets		Liabilities	
Cash	$ 2,500	Accounts Payable	$ 500
Accts. Rec.	5,000	Loans	3,500
Inventory	6,000		$ 4,000
Prepaid Ins.	500	Owner's Equity	$10,000
	$14,000		
Total Assets	$14,000	Total Liab. & Owner's Equity	$14,000

46. *This is what the balance sheet might look like after six months of operation. Note that the owner's equity has increased to $10,000.*

of goods shipped. From this, subtract a percentage for discounts expected to be taken by those who pay early. Large businesses also subtract a percentage for expected bad debts (those they'll never be able to collect).

A similar problem exists with operating expenses. Salaries should only reflect money paid for hours worked during the actual month's period. If you paid your employees on June 3rd for the previous two-week's work, you're including salaries for work that wasn't done in June. Similarly, if your employees won't be paid until July for the last week's work in June, this amount will be missing on your income statement. To rectify this, subtract the over-amount paid June 3rd and add the amount they'd be paid for work in the last week of June.

This principle holds true throughout your operating expenses. In fact to be really accurate, you'd have to take an inventory at the beginning and end of each period to find the amount of materials that were actually used to produce the goods shipped that month.

Since it's time-consuming to be so accurate, we think the standard income statement in Figure 47 is adequate for monthly statements. It will give you a rough idea of your profits and losses by showing the balance between money received that month and money spent. However, once a year take an inventory and make an accurate income statement for the whole year period so you'll know exactly what the business did.

Full-Year Income Statement. In Figure 48, an example of a full-year income statement, the revenues include the actual sales for the whole year, whether or not they've been paid for.

The first two items under "Cost of Goods Sold" are the finished goods and raw materials inventory. Next, list the cost of salaries, freight, tools, materials, and rent, etc., for the year. Total these items, and subtract the finished goods and raw materials inventory to get the total cost of goods sold.

General expenses include items such as sales commissions, office supplies actually used (subtract the cost of any materials still in inventory), bad debts (uncollectable invoices), discounts already taken by customers, and discounts expected to be taken on the remaining accounts receivable. Subtract the general expenses, and you'll get the net income for the year.

Depreciation. If your business purchases include any machinery or equipment that will last for several years, the correct way to itemize these expenses is through depreciation. For example, if you buy a machine for $1,000 and you expect it to last 10 years, only deduct $100.00 each year for its use because you still have $900.00 worth of the machine left after the first year.

To keep track of depreciation expenses, set up two T-accounts (see Figure 49). When you purchase a machine on another piece of equipment, enter it on the debit side of Equipment Purchases and the credit side of Cash. When you write off a percentage of the amount for depreciation at the end of the month or year, enter it in the credit side of Equipment Purchases and the debit side of the Depreciation account.

This Depreciation account is necessary for an accurate picture of your business. If you buy $10,000 worth of machinery in one year that will be used over the next ten, why should this whole $10,000 be subtracted from earnings of the first year? In Chapter 17, Income Taxes, you'll also find that Uncle Sam requires you to use this method. There might be an exception with a used machine whose future life isn't certain. If a machine

Income Statement: 6/1/75 - 6/30/75

	Dollar Cost	Dollar Income
<u>Revenues</u>		$5,000
<u>Operating Expenses</u>		
Salaries	$ 400	
Commissions	500	
Rent	100	
Freight	20	
Utilities	50	
Basic Materials	2,000	
Office Supplies	30	
Tools & Equipment	800	
Misc. Expenses	100	
	$4,000	-$4,000
<u>Net Income</u>		$1,000

47. This monthly income statement for June shows the net income for the month by subtracting operating expenses from revenues.

should become useless before its time, however, you can then allocate the rest of its cost to the last year of its operation.

ANALYZING YOUR INCOME STATEMENT

For this analysis, we'll use the full-year income statement shown in Figure 50. Note that a few items have been added to this statement. This business made $50,000 in wholesale sales and $10,000 by selling at fairs and fleamarkets. Payroll taxes, which are listed separately from salaries, are a definite labor cost because you must pay them if you have employees.

Since this business operates in a state that has general sales tax, the tax has to be paid on all direct sales such as sales from fairs and fleamarkets. The sales tax in this state is 6%; 6% of the $10,000 sales is $600.00, as listed on the statement. The expenses of show fees, traveling, and eating at fairs are also taken into account under "Fair and Fleamarket Expenses."

Figuring Percentages. Notice the percentage listed to the right of each item on the income statement in Figure 50. These percentages were figured by dividing the amount listed for each item by the total amount of sales. For example, to figure the percentage of

Income Statement: 1/1/74 - 12/31/74

	Dollar Cost	Dollar Income
Revenues		$50,000
Cost of Goods Sold		
Finished Goods Inventory 1/1/74	$ 500	
Raw Materials Inventory 1/1/74	2,500	
Salaries	10,000	
Freight	500	
Tools & Equipment	5,000	
Rent	1,200	
Basic Materials	15,000	
	$34,700	
Less Finished Goods Inventory 12/31/74	-300	
Less Raw Materials Inventory 12/31/74	-1,000	
	$33,400	-$33,400
General Expenses		
Sales Commissions	$ 3,000	
Office Supplies	300	
Bad Debts	100	
Discounts	200	
Misc. Expenses	800	
	$4,400	-$ 4,400
Net Income		$12,200

48. A yearly income statement depicts a more accurate measure of the net income by listing beginning and closing inventories for the year.

Equipment Purchases

Date	Item	Debit	Date	Item	Credit	Bal.
2/14	Sewing Machine	$800.00	12/31	depreciation	$76.00	$724.00

Cash

Date	Item	Debit	Date	Item	Credit	Bal.
			2/14	Sewing Machine	$800.00	

Depreciation

Date	Item	Debit	Date	Item	Credit	Bal.
12/31	Sewing Machine	$76.00				$76.00

49. In these three accounts, Equipment Purchases, Cash, and Depreciation, the two transactions show how to record the purchase of a piece of equipment and the depreciation allocation at the end of the year.

salaries, divide $9,000 by $60,000. This percentage tells you that 15% of total revenues were spent on salaries. To get the percentage of total labor costs, add the 15% from salaries to the 5% for payroll taxes to get 20% total labor percentage.

Since the beginning and ending inventories were very close ($2,600 and $2,900), they were not taken into account in figuring these percentages. The total percentage for cost of goods sold was 62.4%. General expenses were 10.15%. The percentage of income or profit was 27.85%.

Value of Percentages. In Chapter 2, on pricing, we showed how this type of analysis can help you develop prices. If raw materials will always be 33% of revenues, you can use this figure in setting prices. If you feel that 33% is too high, perhaps you ought to look for cheaper suppliers, or raise your prices. However, 27.85% is a healthy profit percentage so this business will probably want to use these same percentages in its future activities.

If there's only one owner of the business, and he works full time, he might decide that $16,710 is a fine yearly salary. If two people work at the business full time and split the $16,710, perhaps they'd want to increase their net income the following year. This

Income Statement: 1/1/74 - 12/31/74

	Cost Percentage	Dollar Cost	Dollar Income
Revenues			
Wholesale Sales			$50,000
Fairs & Fleamarkets			10,000
			$60,000
Cost of Goods Sold			
Finished Goods Inventory 1/1/74		$ 600	
Raw Materials Inventory 1/1/74		2,000	
Salaries	15%	9,000	
Payroll Taxes	5%	3,000	
Raw Materials	33%	19,800	
Equipment Depreciation	4%	2,400	
Freight	2.4%	1,440	
Rent	3%	1,800	
	62.4%	$40,040	
Less Finished Goods Inventory 12/31/74		-400	
Less Raw Materials Inventory 12/31/74		-2,500	
		$37,140	-$37,140
General Expenses			
Sales Commissions	5%	$ 3,000	
Office Supplies	1%	600	
Bad Debts	.25%	150	
Discounts	.8%	500	
Sales Taxes	1%	600	
Fair & Fleamarket Expenses	.5%	300	
Misc. Expenses	1.6%	1,000	
	10.15%	$ 6,150	-$ 6,150
Net Income	27.85%		$16,710

can be done by increasing sales and keeping the same profit percentage, or by trying to decrease some of the costs in order to increase the profit percentage. In any case, this type of percentage analysis will show you what has happened in the past and will set a guideline for future spending, pricing, and sales.

WHY BOTHER WITH ANALYSES?

You may wonder if learning all of this is too high a price to pay for having your own business. You're not the least bit interested in bookkeeping or accounting. So why not just hire an accountant? First of all, with the do-it-yourself approach, you'll save a good deal of money, but even more important, you'll be aware of what's going on, particularly in the beginning. Read the accounting books listed in the Bibliography if you want more details on these concepts. Then, if you'd like to have an accountant's expert opinion, hire one to look over your methods of bookkeeping, check your analyses, and offer tax advice.

It's not unusual for a business to fail for lack of financial information. And without such analyses, you can't begin to adjust prices or even know if your business is profitable. Equally important, all loan officers and local, state, and federal tax officials will be asking for information contained in your analyses.

Planning next year's growth is impossible without an accurate rendering of this year's finances. Although business is risky, there's great potential for earning a nice profit. However, risks should be calculated and carefully analyzed. Without such information it's a bit like flying a plane at night without instruments and upside down.

CHECKLIST

1. Total and balance your T-accounts at the end of every month.

2. Each month make a rough income statement showing the money taken in minus the money spent to get the net income or loss.

3. At least once a year make a balance sheet indicating the total assets minus the total liabilities to get the owner's equity.

4. At the end of the year make a full-year income statement with adjustments to indicate actual revenues (beginning of the year inventory minus end of year inventory) minus the cost of goods sold minus general expenses to get the net income or loss.

5. If you purchase machinery and other equipment with useful lives of more than a year, use the depreciation method. Set up a Depreciation T-account and include in full-year income statement.

6. Analyze your full-year income statement by figuring percentages of each item over total revenues (cost ÷ revenues, income ÷ revenues, etc.). Use this analysis for price development, planning future purchases, or sales goals.

50. (Left) This yearly income statement includes cost and profit percentages.

ON THE ROAD

When you sell to friends or neighbors and at fairs or fleamarkets, you're selling directly to your customers. But when you sell on consignment or wholesale to stores, you must convince the owner or buyer of that store that your merchandise will sell in his or her shop. In this chapter we'll discuss the aspects of this type of selling so you'll be prepared to get out on the road in the morning and come back at night with orders.

WHAT TO BRING

There's a tendency in the beginning to want to bring one of every item you make. But remember that you'll be carrying all this around all day long. People don't realize the actual physical labor involved in selling — lugging suitcases full of samples up and down the block and in and out of stores. So carefully choose your best samples and put them into one or two lightweight suitcases.

Put a tag on each sample with an identifying name or number and its wholesale price. This information will come in handy as you show the merchandise to the buyer. In addition, have printed sheets listing these identifying names and/or numbers with prices (they can be printed or mimeographed quite cheaply). A buyer can then use it to order in the future (see Figure 51).

Order Forms. You'll need some type of form on which to write up any orders you get. You can purchase a book of order forms from your local office-supply store. They usually come with carbons so you can make a copy for the store. On the top of each form, print or stamp your name, address, and phone number so the buyer will have this information for easy reference. He'll always want a copy of the order so he has a record of what he purchased.

There are forms you can have imprinted with your name and address that look more professional and are easier to use. You can probably order them from your office-supply store or by mail from Watts Business Forms (see Chapter 4 for the address). Or if you'd like to design your own order forms, you can have them specially printed (although they'll be much more expensive).

January 1974 Wholesale Prices		Per Each	Per Dozen
#210	New Saddle Colors: Natural, Rust/Dk. Brown, Dk. Brown/Black	$12.00	$132.00
#211A	New Round w/Applique Design Colors: Natural, Wheat/ Russet, Red/Burgundy	8.00	90.00
#211B	New Round w/Mushroom Design Colors: Natural, Wheat/ Russet, Mint Green	8.00	90.00
#212A	New Square w/Lace Edge Design Colors: Natural, Rust/Dk. Brown, Wheat/Russet	8.00	90.00
#212B	New Square w/Indian Design Colors: Natural, Wheat/ Russet, Rust/Dk. Brown	8.00	90.00
#213A	Junior w/Flower Design Colors: White, Natural, Blue, Burgundy	6.50	72.00
#213B	Junior w/Indian Design Colors: White, Natural, Wheat/Russet	6.50	72.00
#214A	Big Junior w/Flower Design Colors: White, Natural, Blue, Burgundy	8.00	90.00
#214B	Big Junior w/Indian Design Colors: White, Natural, Wheat/Russet	8.00	90.00
#215A	Box Bag w/Dog Design Colors: Natural, Wheat/ Russet	5.00	54.00

51. This page of our Holy Cow Leather wholesale price list shows how each item is given an identifying number and name.

Filling Out an Order Form. In Figure 52, a sample order, the purchase order number was written in, but you can also get order forms with consecutive numbers already printed on them. In the block next to "To," the billing name and address is listed. Be certain to get the complete address, including the zip code, and also get the phone number. After "Ship To" put "same," or list the shipping address if it's different.

If the customer has his own order number, print this number here. Under "Shipping Date" write in the expected delivery time, such as two weeks or 10 days. Under "Ship Via" list the shipping method, such as UPS or parcel post. If the customer has a preferred way, discuss it with him when writing up the order. It's not necessary to fill in "Salesman" unless there are several people selling. Write in the terms agreed on (see Chapter 4) so the buyer knows whether to expect credit, a discount, C.O.D., etc.

Under "Quantity" write in the amount of each item ordered. Be sure to put "each" or "dozen" so this will be clear. Under "Description," make sure you give enough information so you'll know exactly what to ship later and your customers will know exactly what they ordered. Under "Unit Price" list the price for each or per dozen. Some salespeople don't fill in the extended "Amount" at the time of writing up the order. They prefer to do it back at the office so they can use a calculator to check their arithmetic. But often a buyer wants you to extend the amount and total the order so he'll know how much he spent. A pocket calculator will come in handy here.

Other information you may want to list on the order is credit information (such as names and addresses of references) and banks. Also be sure to have the buyer sign the order at the bottom of the form. If you can't read the signature, print it yourself for future reference. Now tear off a copy and give it to him.

Miscellaneous Items. Bring several pens or pencils and a scratch pad for taking notes. Business cards are a good idea and inexpensive to have printed (see Figure 54). We use a standard white card, but you can get them in all colors and with any type of design. Some people feel that an unusual business card attracts attention and helps a buyer remember who you are. We feel that our name alone is unusual enough to make them remember us.

A clipboard is handy for writing up orders. Keep it ready with a new order set clipped in so you'll be ready to write it up. A manilla folder keeps your written orders together and out of the sight of your next customers. Use an attaché case for holding order forms, clipboard, pens, price sheets, etc.

A catalog or other advertising literature is great to have, but not always feasible. It gets expensive to have color catalogs printed so perhaps you could make a simple catalog by drawing pictures in ink and having them printed or mimeographed (see Figure 53). By leaving a catalog sheet and price list with a customer; even though he doesn't order at the time, he may order later on.

YOUR FIRST DAY SELLING

We suggest that the first time you sell, go to a local shopping area and approach stores you're familiar with. Since you've shopped in them or at least heard of them, you'll know what kind of merchandise they carry. Perhaps you even know some of the buyers or owners personally. Figure out which ones will be most likely to carry your product, and start there.

In general, craft shops, galleries, and gift stores will be the places most craftspeople

Phone - 274-6607

Holy Cow Leather
180 HORTON ROAD
NEWFIELD, N.Y. 14867
TEL. - 607-564-9022

Purchase Order No. **304**

TO ⌐ The Sun Shop
24 MAIN ST.
Anywhere, N.Y. 10001 ⌐

SHIP TO ⌐ SAME ⌐

CUST'S ORDER NO.	SHIPPING DATE	SHIP VIA		SALESMAN	TERMS
A215	10 DAYS	UPS		LYN	1% 10 Net 30

QUANTITY	DESCRIPTION	UNIT PRICE	AMOUNT
1 DZ	1 3/4" belts, Assorted	42.00	42.00
2 ea	#213A Junior w/flower, white + blue	6.50	13.00
3 ea	#215B Box Bag w/cat, all Natural	5.00	15.00
			70.00
	Dun + Bradstreet		
	Sun County Bank		
	Mary Smith		
	(MARY SMITH)		

WILCO BUSINESS FORMS, INC., ITHACA, N.Y. S/F NO. 100

52. *Our Holy Cow Leather order form is a standard form that we had imprinted with our name and address.*

Holy Cow Leather

180 HORTON ROAD
NEWFIELD, NEW YORK 14867

PHONE: (607) 564 - 9022

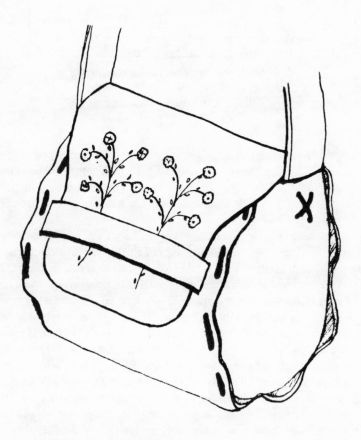

```
Style #213A  JUNIOR w/Flower Design (As Shown)
Colors:  White, Natural, Blue, Burgundy

Style #213B  JUNIOR w/Indian Design
Colors:  White, Natural, Wheat/Russet
```

53. This ad sheet, printed from an ink drawing, is much cheaper than color sheets and will still remind the customer what your product looks like.

54. Although our business card is very plain,
it gives all the necessary information.

will try to sell to. If you make leather goods, jewelry, or clothing, you might also try boutique shops, and clothing stores. If you make belts or handbags, shoe stores will be worth investigating. In the beginning we tried any store we thought might possibly sell our goods. But after awhile you'll learn to choose the kinds of stores that are best for you.

The Initial Approach. If you have business cards, keep a few in your coat pocket and have one in your hand as you walk in the door. Tell the first free clerk who you are, where you're from, and mention that you'd like to see the owner or buyer. The clerk usually looks at the card and says he's the buyer, he'll get the buyer, or the buyer isn't in.

Once the buyer is in front of you, explain briefly who you are and what you'd like to show him. Be courteous and friendly and smile. Tell the buyer you'll only take a few minutes and get him to look at an article as quickly as possible. In fact, if you can keep one small sample in your pocket or another handy place, take it out immediately so he can see the fine quality, attractiveness, and workmanship.

Buyers' Responses. Expect all kinds of responses. Some buyers will say they're too busy now to see you. If so, ask when you can come again at a better time. Others will immediately say they're not interested in what you have. Others will stand there saying nothing, watching you go through your whole presentation, and then say they just don't have a call for your type of merchandise. Others will say they already have something just like it, or cheaper, or there's no room in their shop, or they've spent their Christmas money already, etc.

As long as they're looking, keep showing your merchandise, and talk about the quality and workmanship, how well they've sold in a similar shop in the next town, how low your prices are compared to similar quality merchandise, and how unusual your things are. You might explain that you have no minimum first order and would be happy to place a few things with him so he can try them out. Often your enthusiasm for the products you've worked on and designed yourself will go a long way toward convincing a prospective buyer. Often the goods sell themselves and all you have to do is get the buyer to look at them.

Approaching a New Town. After you've exhausted familiar shopping areas, check a map of your state and choose the most populated areas within driving distance. Start out early in the morning with your samples. When you reach the first town, drive around slowly on the main streets to find the central shopping area with the most shops. Then park your car at one end of the main area or street.

As you walk up the block, go into every store that might possibly handle your merchandise. Don't stand outside looking in the window wondering if they're right for you or not. We've sold to many stores that appeared to be an unlikely prospect from the outside. Anyway, you won't waste more than a few words and minutes if you've chosen the wrong place. Don't be afraid to be turned down. Smile, say "thanks anyway," and leave. Or ask if you may leave your card in case the buyer is interested at a later date. Cover the whole area up and down the block, and end up back at your car.

Laying the Groundwork. Don't feel that you've wasted your time because your first trip to a particular town netted no actual sales. Often it takes two or more visits before a store can be sold on your goods. By showing your product, talking to people, and leaving literature and price lists, they're gradually getting to know you and your company. You may have come at a time when the store has no extra money in its budget for purchasing new items. Or perhaps the store never carried anything similar to your line before. Maybe at a future date they'll decide to try it.

Sometimes a buyer isn't able to make the decision himself. If he's not the owner of the store, he may have to get the owner's approval before making the actual purchase. Sometimes buyers want to sit on the decision before purchasing a new product. When they see you coming back regularly, they begin to believe you're a reliable source and become more willing to take a chance with you.

In the beginning, we found a great fear on buyers' parts that we wouldn't come through with delivery, or stay in business long enough to serve them on a regular basis. Stores want regular suppliers they can count on. They can't sit around waiting for you to get inspired while their shelves are empty. So one of your big selling jobs is to convince them you're reliable and will produce the goods.

GETTING INFORMATION

Keep a small pad and pencil handy at all times. If you go into a store and the buyer is out, ask for his name and telephone number. Jot this information down so you can call and make an appointment for a later date. Ask the clerk questions about the possibility of your merchandise selling in the store, and if he thinks the buyer would be interested.

Another question to ask in a new town is where other shopping centers are located. Or if a store tells you they don't carry that type of merchandise, ask if they know of any stores in the area that might.

As you leave each store, make a note of what happened. Title a page in your notebook with the name of the town and the date. Then write down the name of the store you just went to and list what happened: "not interested in this type of merchandise," "buyer out of town – will be back Tuesday," "come back in two months," etc. Also write the names of owners or buyers and their phone numbers.

Sometimes you'll walk into chain stores, or stores with branches located in different towns or states. Usually all their buying is done from a home office, so ask for the name and address. You can never tell when this information will come in handy.

ADVANCE APPOINTMENTS

Once you've developed a notebook full of names, addresses, and phone numbers, on your next visit to town you can call in advance and make appointments. You can save yourself a lot of time and running around if you find out in advance what day the buyer will be able to see you. Some buyers have very tight schedules and will only see sales-people by appointment. But even those with more time may be out of town occasionally.

If you're going to try the buyers of large chain or department stores, you must make appointments first. Since some buyers designate certain days for sales representatives, we'll try to give you an idea of what to expect on that day. When you walk in at 9:00 you're given a number in the order of your arrival and are told to set up your samples in a certain booth. The buyer arrives, moves from booth to booth seeing different representatives, and quickly dismisses those he or she isn't interested in. In general, the larger the outfit and the bigger the city, the colder, more formal, and tougher-skinned the buyers are. When you have an appointment with one of them, make sure you know exactly what you're talking about and can answer any question that might come up.

ATTITUDE

It takes a certain attitude to be a good salesperson. If you've never done any selling before you may find it a fearful thing. But by using your most pleasant and polite manner, you'll be amazed to discover that most people will be nice in return, and perhaps even compliment your merchandise. You'll find that after the first two or three sales it isn't as terrible as you thought.

Some people take naturally to selling — they simply enjoy being on the road and meeting new people. If you're like this, you have nothing to worry about. But if you're not this type, you have to force yourself in the beginning to just get out and do it. Make yourself go into every possible store up and down every block in every town with shops. After awhile you'll get used to the no's and won't mind them. You'll be able to enjoy the people you encounter, talk more easily about your products, and come up with good answers to questions.

Remember, you have a good product. When a store carries it and sells it, they make money also. They aren't doing you a big favor by buying your merchandise; it's a mutually advantageous situation. The more of your merchandise they sell, the more money both of you make. You're bringing a potential money-making product into every store you enter. Keep this in mind at all times and your attitude will be fine.

CHECKLIST

1. Choose samples from your product line and tag each one with the item name and/or number and price.

2. Pack bags: samples, order forms, pens and/or pencils, scratch pad, business cards, clipboard, price sheets, catalog or ad sheets, manilla folder.

3. Start selling to stores in your own area, especially if you know the owners or sales-people.

4. When you walk into a new store, introduce yourself and ask to see the buyer. Try to present at least one item quickly to get him or her interested in looking at all your samples.

5. While showing your goods, make these basic points: describe each item, and point out the workmanship and quality; point out why these products will sell in this store and explain how prices compare with competition; point out that you have no minimum first order, and close by asking buyer to try a few items in his or her shop because you're sure they'll sell.

6. Check your state map to line up either towns and cities within driving distance. When entering a new town, drive around first, then park and walk up and down the block, going into every shop that might possibly buy.

7. Get all the information you can — keep a notebook listing name of each store, what happened, buyers' names, telephone numbers, etc.

8. Make advance appointments whenever possible, and always with big department stores or chains.

9. Don't expect to make every sale on the first visit. Keep going back to stores that show the slightest interest.

10. Develop a positive attitude. You're offering every store you walk into a chance to buy merchandise that will make it money. You know you have a good product, and you should keep this in mind at all times.

CONSIGNMENT VS. WHOLESALE

In "wholesale" selling, once a store signs an order it has committed itself to accept these goods when you ship them at the prices listed on the order form. If the terms are C.O.D., it must pay for the goods immediately on delivery. If there are other terms, it has agreed to abide by them. Once the goods have been shipped they're owned by the store. The store can now sell them for any price it desires, although the usual markup is 100%.

When a store takes your merchandise on "consignment," however, it means they won't pay for anything until it's sold. You determine the retail price of each item, and the store takes a percentage of that price when the item is sold. For instance, if you price a pot at $10.00 retail and the store has a consignment percentage of 30%, when the pot is sold you'll get $7.00 and the store $3.00. So a $10.00 retail item would net you $7.00 on consignment, or $5.00 by selling wholesale. If the consignment percentage was less, say 20%, you'd make even more money.

THE PRO'S AND CON'S

Let's say you give a store $100.00 worth of merchandise on consignment on a 30% basis. This is worth $30.00 to the store and $70.00 to you, but *only* after the merchandise is sold. If nothing sells the first month, then you receive no money that month. It could take a year for you to get your $70.00 and it's even possible that some items won't sell at all. Then again, you might find a store that sells $100.00 worth of your merchandise every month and sends you a check regularly.

We recommend consignment selling as a way to begin selling to small shops on a small scale. This way you can avoid some of the pressures of short delivery schedules, high volume production, and wholesale competitive pricing. You can test out different stores to see which are the best places to carry your product. You'll also have a chance to experiment with new items, work out the kinks, and seek out better suppliers. As long as you take precautions and keep proper records, there's no reason why consignment selling can't be a profitable way for a small craft business to market its product.

THE CONSIGNMENT CONTRACT

To set up a consignment account, some sort of contract or agreement is necessary. You want to be sure that both you and the store agree on the terms on which you'll leave your merchandise (see Figure 55).

In the first sentence of the contract the store acknowledges the receipt of a certain amount of merchandise on a specific date at a standard percentage rate. That's the basic agreement. However, you also want to know that you're going to receive your money on a regular basis. There are many loose arrangements where the craftsperson just comes by once in a while to see if anything was sold and to collect his money. But unless the shop is in your home town, it will become bothersome to keep checking up on every store where you have consignment merchandise. You can save yourself a lot of running around by having the store send you a check every month along with a list of what was sold and requests for more merchandise. Any *good* consignment account will do this for you.

However, don't forget about an account completely and never stop in to see them. It's important to get a feel for the type of store, to offer display suggestions, and to see what particular items sell best. Also, you may find that a store you haven't heard from in six months is closed when you get there — they've gone out of business and taken your goods with them.

Removal Option Clause. The next part of the contract gives the store the option of having you take back your merchandise if it doesn't sell. A store owner doesn't want to take up shelf space with goods that don't sell, and it doesn't do you any good to have them there, either. So if a month or two goes by without sales, this option clause allows you to pick up the goods after notifying the store 10 days in advance. The 10 days gives the store a chance to replace your merchandise with someone else's. Finally, if the store refuses to cooperate and won't send you checks when you know merchandise has been sold, you can pick up your goods without notifying them.

The Value of Precautions. You may wonder why all these precautions are necessary. Shouldn't you be able to trust a store to handle things fairly? Probably most will. But the reason a store takes merchandise on consignment in the first place is usually because it's small, it hasn't been in business long, and it doesn't have the financial backing to buy goods wholesale. If a store is having difficulty paying the rent each month, it may not be too prompt in paying consignment sales. You're only a small supplier. If a shop is under pressure, it will pay its rent and big suppliers first because it can't exist without them.

New, small shops are constantly opening up and by the same token they're constantly closing down. If a shop closes or goes bankrupt, it may be impossible to collect your money. Therefore it's important to watch a new consignment shop carefully. Begin by giving them a few items to see if they can sell the merchandise and if they pay promptly. Once you've dealt with them successfully for a few months you can trust them with more merchandise.

We have some very good consignment accounts that send us checks regularly. They let us know what items they're running low on and we send or bring them more. With each check they give us a listing of what items they've sold. Once in awhile we stop in to talk about new items, price changes, and display. But we've also had stores that we've never heard from again once we left the merchandise. Finally, after many calls and letters we received the check for sold goods that was due us. One shop closed down without ever contacting us and when we tried to call, we found that their phone had been discon-

Consignment Agreement

Bubbles Boutique, 666 Main Street, Ourtown, USA, received the following merchandise from Clever Crafts on September 9, 1973 at a consignment rate of 30%. A check for all sales will be sent to Clever Crafts the first of each month for goods sold the previous month. After one month from above date, Bubbles Boutique may notify Clever Crafts to remove goods for any reason. Clever Crafts may also pick up any unsold goods after one month for any reason after notifying Bubbles Boutique 10 days in advance. If checks for sold items are not forthcoming monthly, Clever Crafts may remove goods without 10 days notice. Bubbles Boutique will be responsible for goods while in their shop -- that is, for fire, theft, etc.

Description of Item	Retail Price Each	Total
10 wide belts	$10.00	$100.00
10 skinny belts	5.00	50.00
12 barrettes	2.00	24.00
		$174.00

CLEVER CRAFTS   BUBBLES BOUTIQUE

55. This is a typical agreement between your craft business and the store that's taking your goods on consignment.

nected. Finally, a couple of letters brought some response and we were given an address where we could pick up the merchandise — none of which had been sold.

Fire, Theft Clause. We added the last sentence to the contract after we experienced such a problem ourselves. In the fall a relatively new shop took some of our merchandise on consignment. By Christmas they had reordered many times and were doing very well with it. In January we called them to see if they needed more stock and they told us a sad story about how the shop had been robbed. At that time we didn't have the last sentence in our agreement. Legally, we could have been responsible for the merchandise since we still owned it. Of course, the obvious question is how much was stolen and how much did the store really sell? Since the store didn't keep very good records, they probably didn't even know. As it turns out, however, they finally agreed to take the loss.

You may find that some stores will refuse to agree to this clause and instead ask you to sign a release saying they won't be responsible for loss, fire, or theft of your merchandise while it's in their store. It's our feeling that since you have no control over the way the owners run their store, they should be responsible for the merchandise once you leave it with them. One store owner refused to sign our agreement because of this final sentence, so we didn't leave our merchandise with him. If a store refuses to be responsible, you'll have to make the same decision.

CONSIGNMENT NOTEBOOK

Good bookkeeping is another important aspect of consignment transactions. Before leaving a box of merchandise with a store, make sure you have an accurate list of everything in it. Have the store sign for receipt of all merchandise, especially in initial dealings.

It's a good idea to set up a consignment notebook to keep track of all these transactions (use a looseleaf notebook because you can add pages).

Recording Transactions. Divide each sheet into columns as shown in Figure 56. On the left, enter the date of the transaction and the name of the item. Under "Store Received," put the amount of that item left with the store. Under "Sold," list the number sold by the store. Under "Returned," put the amount of the item the store returned to you, if any. Under "Remaining," put the amount the store still has. "Remaining" should equal "Store Received" minus "Sold" and "Returned." For example, the first time you leave a box of goods with a store, fill in the date you left the goods and then list each item (see Figure 57).

Suppose a month later the store sends you a check for $24.10 and gives you a list of four items sold. Record that transaction in the manner shown in Figure 58.

The following month you stop at the store and show them some new items, let's say ashtrays. They take six of them and also ask you to take back two large vases that they feel won't sell in their store. Figure 59 shows how to record that transaction.

Cash Received Records. Besides the regular accounting of merchandise, it's good to keep a record of the actual cash amount received each month from a store. Set up a second notebook page like the one in Figure 60.

Each month, list whether or not you received a check under "Date." In the "Cash Received" column, list the amount of each check received. In the "Total Received" column, keep a cumulative total — that is, add each month's check to the previous total.

Date	Item	Received	Sold	Returned	Remaining

56. *Here's a way of setting up your consignment notebook to keep track of your transactions with the store.*

Date	Item	Received	Sold	Returned	Remaining
6/7	planters	4			
	casseroles	6			
	tea pot sets	3			
	large vases	2			
	small vases	6			

57. *This shows how your notebook might look the first time you leave your crafts on consignment with a store.*

Date	Item	Received	Sold	Returned	Remaining
6/7	planters	4			
	casseroles	6			
	tea pot sets	3			
7/7	casseroles		2		4
	tea pot sets		1		2

58. This is how your entry might look a month later, after the same store has sold some of your crafts.

Date	Item	Received	Sold	Returned	Remaining
6/7	planters	4			
	casseroles	6			
	tea pot sets	3			
	large vases	2			
7/7	casseroles		2		4
	tea pot sets		1		2
8/7	large vases			2	0
	ashtrays	6			

59. Here you can see how further transactions, including the return of unsold items, are entered in the consignment notebook.

Date	Cash Received	Total Received

60. It's a good idea to record separately the actual amount of money received from the store each month in your consignment notebook.

This useful record shows just how much business a store is doing for you, and helps determine whether a store is worth dealing with. If several months go by without a check, you'd better find out what's wrong.

WHOLESALE SELLING

In order to sell wholesale, you must be able to make a profit by selling your merchandise at 50% of the retail price (see Chapter 2, Pricing). Your profit percentage may be less than you make on consignment, but hopefully with larger orders and more sales, it will be worth it in the long run.

When you're ready to move into larger production and want to increase your total sales, it's time to sell wholesale. Anyway, all stores except for the small craft shop or gallery will deal with you *only* on a wholesale basis. So if you want to sell to larger stores, you'll have to sell wholesale.

Requirements. First of all, your wholesale prices must be low enough so that when doubled, the merchandise will be at a price low enough to attract customers. Some stores will mark up more than 100%, especially large chains and department stores. Therefore, they'll want your merchandise at even lower prices than a single, small shop would. You may want to develop two sets of prices, one for small orders and one for volume orders. Use the volume price sheet only when dealing with large stores and chains who buy in these quantities.

Second, you must offer dependable, quick delivery. Six months, for instance, isn't a very good delivery schedule. We try to stick to two weeks, and we've even had complaints about that at times. It's very frustrating, but it seems that when a store finally decides they want your merchandise, they want it yesterday — especially around Christmas. No store wants an order they placed in September to be delivered December 1st. They want the merchandise in their store for the whole two or three months of Christmas shopping.

Third, the merchandise you ship must exactly duplicate the samples you've shown the buyer. If the goods you end up sending are of poorer quality, different materials, or different sizes, you're going to find it very difficult to get a reorder from that store. And since you want it to get there in tip-top shape, you must pack the order with enough care so it arrives complete and without damage (see Chapter 4, Shipping).

SUMMING UP

You'll find there are pro's and con's to each method of selling. Consignment will allow you to get your product into a small store that doesn't have a lot of money to buy all of its goods, although you may have to wait quite some time before receiving payment. The store may even be so under-capitalized that it will go out of business and you'll never find the owner or your goods again.

On the other hand, wholesale selling gives you a little less per item but the advantage is that you get paid by a set date, the orders are larger, and the store is often more reliable in paying for what it orders. We look upon consignment as a first step — a way to get your craft into shops when just beginning your business. Wholesale, then, is the "big time." You're able to produce more, you want to sell more, and in order to plan and budget your own expenditures, you want to estimate more accurately when payments will be coming in. Once you've reached this second growth stage we see no reason to continue with consignment selling except perhaps to a friend's craft shop, or to an unusually active shop with a record of fast turnover of your goods and regular payments.

CHECKLIST

1. In consignment selling, you own the merchandise while it's in the store. The store takes a percentage from 10% to 33% and pays you when the products are sold.

2. In wholesale selling the store buys the merchandise from you at 50% of the retail price — they own the goods once they're shipped, and they can sell them for any price they choose.

3. Consignment is useful when you start out, and you're selling to small craft shops, gift stores, and galleries.

4. Prepare a consignment contract and always have the store sign it.

5. Take the precautions of a removal option clause and a fire and theft clause.

6. Keep a consignment notebook to help you keep track of transactions.

7. Keep in touch with consignment stores regularly to make sure they're still in business, to find out if any items have sold, and to pick up checks or merchandise.

8. Move into wholesale selling when you're ready to increase sales and sell to larger stores.

10

FAIRS-
AND NOT
SO FAIR

The sun is a-shining
  to welcome the day,
With a high-ho,
  come to the fair.

Old English Folk Song

Despite the words of the song, the sun isn't always a-shining at the fair. Sometimes the rain soaks your macramé, or the wind blows your pottery off the stand and you wish you hadn't signed up for the fair. Sometimes you even vow never to go to another fair.

Why then have we gone to them time after time? The definition of a fair will provide a simple answer — a craft fair is a group of craftspeople who are gathered together to display and sell their products to others interested in their wares. This logic encourages us to go to the next one, particularly in view of the fact that Jim, who does horseshoe-nail wall hangings, said he sold out last year at this very same fair! Well if Jim did so well, we'll go too.

FINDING FAIRS

There are several types of fairs you may be interested in. County and state fairs are usually held once a year in the summer. A booklet by Margaret Chaiet (22500 Vanowen Street, Canoga Park, Ca. 91304, $2.00) lists dates, places, names, and addresses of state, county, and regional fairs throughout the U.S. These fairs usually include livestock shows, stock car or thrill shows, rides, entertainment, food, and many other general exhibits. Crafts are usually just a small part of such a fair, and therefore it could be a total waste of time, as we found it to be. But we've also heard of craftspeople doing quite well at state fairs. The best way to check it out is to go to one and talk to the craftspeople who exhibit there. Notice how many customers go into the crafts tent, and how many sales are made during a particular period of time. Then, if you think it may be worthwhile, give it a try. County fairs will probably have reasonable fees for exhibiting, about $20.00 for a 10 X 10 foot space, but state fairs may run $300.00 or higher for a booth.

Another kind of fair is a fleamarket, where mostly old junk and antiques are sold. Often a fleamarket is run by professionals who own a piece of property along a highway and charge space fees from $4.00 to $20.00 for you to set up shop. They provide a food concession and are supposed to do some advertising. Look for fleamarkets along the highway and watch your local paper for advertisements. It might be worth while to try one for a day. First, talk to people who exhibit regularly and ask them about peak seasons and best days of the week.

Another type of fair is really an art show, and is usually run by painters or sculptors. There are many art organizations that run such events, and lately they've been allowing craftspeople to exhibit with them. A problem arises, however, because basically they're equipped to exhibit paintings, not crafts. Painters often don't expect to sell much at an exhibit, so what they call a great show may prove to be a bomb for you. They also tend to forget to advertise crafts and neglect adequate display provisions for crafts. You can find these groups by checking with museums, watching your newspaper, and talking to artists.

The real, down-to-earth *craft* fair, set up solely for the exhibit and sale of crafts, will probably be the best type to go to. The only problem is that there are so many of them. They're run by churches, Y's, 4-H Clubs, chambers of commerce, and professional groups. Once you know about them, you could undoubtedly set yourself up from spring to fall with a fair to go to every weekend. The trick is to weed out the bad ones and get to all the good ones.

The best way to find out about craft fairs, once you've checked with the chamber of commerce, newspapers, etc., is to go to a fair and talk to the craftspeople. Ask if they know about any other fairs; give them your name and address, and ask them to send you the pertinent information when they get home. Take their names and addresses and promise to send them any information you have. You'll soon build up quite a list, and eventually you'll get your name on mailing lists. Some states or regional areas may have a service that lists all the local craft fairs, but craftspeople are generally very good about sharing such information.

Finally, there are some professional shows that include painters as well as crafts-people. They have standard forms, fees, restrictions, etc., that you must follow. Once you get on their mailing lists you'll receive notices about all their upcoming fairs. Listed below are three professional organizations we know of:

Jinx Harris Shows, Inc.
RFD 1, Box 153 J
Auburn, N.H. 03032

L. Koerner
21 Fowler Ave., R-2
Peekskill, N.Y. 10566

American Crafts Expositions
P.O. Box 274
Farmington, Conn. 06032

What to Look For. Some fairs have specific restrictions, for example, all wares must be the original work of the exhibitor. Other fairs will allow anyone to sell anything. Fleamarkets usually have more old junk and antiques being sold than handcrafted items. Finding out in advance what the majority of exhibits will be is very important. If a group of painters is running the show for themselves, they very likely haven't advertised the show to include crafts and haven't provided adequate display areas for crafts. If you go to a fleamarket where most of the exhibitors are selling antiques, this is probably what the customer is coming to buy. Once we sat in the hot sun all day at a fleamarket and sold $15.00 worth of leather goods. Many customers came by, but they spent their money on great-grandma's cut-glass bowl.

Be sure to note what days of the week the fair will be held. In general, Friday night and Saturday are the best times for sales. Sunday can be good, but often people go with the family for an outing, to look only. On Saturday people are accustomed to going shopping, and will bring money. Holidays such as Labor Day or Fourth of July can also be good. The days to avoid are weekdays. As far as the time of year goes – pre-Christmas will always produce a good fair. Any fall fair will probably be better than one held in the middle of the summer. If the day turns out to be blistering hot, your customers are more likely to go to a beach or lake than a crowded fair.

Some things the fair managers will rarely, if ever, tell you are: what the weather will be like, how they've advertised the fair, how many people really came last year, and how many of those people actually bought something. And last but not least – how much of *your* kind of craft sold. If you can, aside from predicting the weather two months away, try to find out some of these more important facts. The only way we've been able to discover the good fairs is to go to as many as we can and try to discover which ones are as good as the promoters say.

By going to the fairs you also find out about things like location. For instance, is it better for you to be near the food concession, near the door, or in the center? Some fairs are held in a large room where people can easily walk around and see everyone. Other fairs are held in buildings with many small rooms, which can be disastrous if you're stuck in a little room that the crowd can't find. However, in a small outside fair all locations will probably be equally good. In a large, rambling fair there may be areas that are more easily accessible. The only way to find these things out is through experience, although word-of-mouth from people who have gone in the past may help. As a general rule, we like to be near heavy traffic areas, so if you can stand the fumes and odors, a spot near the hamburger stand may be profitable.

The Fair Contract. Once you get the name of the group running the fair, write and tell them about your craft. You'll probably get a return letter consisting of anything from a hand-written note to a two-page contract telling you the details of the fair. Included will be information concerning the amount of space, whether to bring tables and chairs, if it's indoors or out, the location, the time, parking, and food. Figure 61 shows a simple form from a small local fair and Figure 62 shows one from a professional fair organization. As you can see, the professional group offers much more information about the fair, plus more stringent requirements that the craftsperson must adhere to.

Signing Up. Once we've decided to go to a fair, we sign the contract, make out a check (if it's a flat fee for the table space) and send it in. Some fairs charge no advance fee for space, but take a percentage of what you sell instead – anywhere from 4% to 30%.

Second Annual Nine Mile Pt. Arts & Crafts Show

The second annual Nine Mile Pt. Arts & Crafts Show, sponsored by the Studio Gallery, Webster, N.Y., will be held at Hedges Nine Mile Pt. Restaurant, Webster, on August 19, 1973 (rain date August 26) from noon until 7:00 PM. A hot dog stand and other refreshments will be on sale to the public.

Registration: $10.00 No Juries, No Commissions

Hanging space for artists and tables for craftsmen will be provided for those who do not have their own display method.

- -

Registration Form

Enclosed is check or money order for $10.00 made payable to the Studio Gallery.

Name: _____

Address: _____

City & State: _____ Zip: _____ Phone: _____

Please check: ____Fine Art   ____Craft

               ____Your display   ____Gallery display

Please Return To: The Studio Gallery   Please return
                    15 W. Main St.   on or before
                    Webster, N.Y. 14580   Aug. 4, 1973.
                    872-6135

Artist Agreement: I agree that Hedges Restaurant and the Studio Gallery, both of Webster, N.Y., shall not be responsible for any loss or damage to art work or personal property of any kind. Sales tax is my responsibility. I will keep my display up until the close of the show.

61. This typical fair contract gives you the necessary information about the fair and provides a registration form to fill out and return.

1st Annual Professional Craft & Sculpture Show
Exton Mall - Exton, Pa.

Sept. 19-22, 1973

<u>Entries</u> - Open to all professional sculptors and craftsmen. All work must be the work of the exhibitor. All work must be original -- No commercial molds in any media -- No paper or plastic flowers. Paintings on wood, découpage, batik, enamel paintings, and dried or pressed flowers will be considered crafts. All exhibitors are encouraged to work on the show. Electrical outlets will be provided for working craftsmen. No one else may use electricity unless battery operated. All tables must be covered on all sides -- to the floor. SUPPLY YOUR OWN TABLES & RACKS. All exhibitors must exhibit during the complete hours of the show. Anyone leaving a show before closing will be taken off the mailing list and refused entrance in any future shows. Work left up at night -- bring a covering for it. Découpage only if $5.00 and up. All exhibitors must be set up by 11 AM first day of show.

<u>Fees</u> - $25.00 for an 8 foot space for all. A space is one 8 ft. table or one 8 ft. rack. A second table, L-shaped will be $10.00 -- maximum space -- three tables set in a U-shape ($45.00) or two tables and one rack $45.00. No refunds after closing date -- Sept. 10, 1973.

<u>Directions</u> - Pa. Pike - Downingtown Exit, Rt. 100 South (about 2 miles), left on Rt. 30, Mall is on the left.

Neither the Exton Mall, the Exton Mall Merchant's Association, the Director, or committee is responsible for loss or damage of work -- all care will be taken.

- -

Reservation - 1st Annual Exton Mall Professional Craft & Sculpture Show - September 19-22, 1973

Name: _____ Spaces: _____

Address: _____ Amt. Enclosed: _____

City: _____ State: _____ Zip: _____

_____ Sculptor_____ Craftsman _____Type (be specific)

62. A contract for a professional fair includes detailed, specific requirements you must follow if you plan to attend.

If you sell $80.00 worth of goods at a 10% fair, you'd pay the promoters $8.00 in commissions. We used to feel that a commission arrangement like this would assure us of good advertising and therefore of good attendance. After all, the more we sell, the more the promoters make. But alas, they tend to have little foresight and tight budgets. Although the old adage, "it takes money to make money" is still generally true, they often don't have or aren't willing to spend much money for advertising. To ensure good attendance, people in the fair area should read about it days in advance, should hear about it repeatedly on their radios, and should even see it on television. The very best fairs may have established a good reputation over the years, but even these must let the public know the date, time, and place of this years' fair.

Acceptance of your application to show your craft at the fair isn't automatic. Good fairs, and even some mediocre ones, frequently select a limited number of craftspeople in any one medium. You may also find that the fair is already filled because you were late in applying. Some fairs are in such demand that you can only get your name on a waiting list for the following year — and good fairs can be worth it. A craft business, like any other, takes time to establish. Thinking ahead and planning for the future is the part of the game that provides the hope and optimism to stick with it, and to expect bigger and better sales over the horizon.

Juried Fairs. Another reason for rejecting your application is that your work doesn't meet the standards of a craft jury. Such fairs, called juried or judged fairs (and so listed in the application form), create a panel of "experts" to review samples of your work prior to acceptance. You may not feel that an expert in watercolor or pottery is *able* to evaluate your stained glass, or even your pottery, but you have little say in the matter. The expert looks at your work, notes the quality of workmanship, and makes a decision. We've often found, however, that more than the judgment of quality goes into his decision. For instance, does he like your materials, your design, or even your colors? One such expert told us brown was in, blue was out. We had been selling blue wholesale and at other fairs three to one over brown, and since this was a commissioned fair (30%), we honestly felt the fair would lose income by rejecting our blues. The judge then stated that money wasn't the object — he was there to "educate the public" to buy brown, no matter what they preferred! This same judge and his cohorts then explained that they really had too many craftspeople and too many items and had to eliminate some, just for space. Clearly these judges' main motive was to make space, and the decision-making was fairly arbitrary. We put up with this, however, because at the same fair the previous year we had just about sold out.

Legitimate Judging. We feel that quality workmanship is a legitimate requirement at any fair. To allow the display of products poorly made from cheap materials lowers the quality and image of the group as a whole. For this reason some promoters list specific requirements for various crafts, such as the list in Figure 63. These are the basic standards for the Washington Square Outdoor Art Exhibits held in Greenwich Village each year.

However, judging the quality of design, like any value judgment, will vary with the person doing the judging. Don't let a disappointing judgment or two get you down. Try to pick out the useful information that will help you improve your product, and try again.

Basic Standards For All Craft Exhibits

Jewelry - Work must be clean, of original design and functional. All metal to metal joints must be soldered, other materials must be riveted, set, or epoxied. Bezels and stone mountings should be formed by the craftsman. All castings must be of the artist's own design.

Plastics - All above jewelry standards apply. Transparent plastics must contain necessary additives to prevent degradation by ultraviolet light. Objects poured in commercial molds not acceptable. Laminating metals, organic matter, pictures or art objects etc. not made by craftsman are prohibited.

Glass - General standards apply.

Ceramics - Edges and seams must be trimmed smooth and sharp projections from stilt marks, blistering, crawling, etc., must be ground smooth. Non-vitreous objects must be glazed and fired to maturity and must serve the purpose for which they were made, i.e., vases, cups, creamers, etc., shall hold liquids and there must be no seepage of liquids into body. Slip-cast or pressed objects from commercial molds not permitted.

Batik - Colors shall be non-bleeding. Tie-dyeing not acceptable.

Leather - Findings and leather edges must have clean finishes. Exterior stitching must be handstitching. All designs must be original. No assemblage of prestamped kits permitted. Only first quality leather may be used. All dyes must be colorfast.

Papier Mâché - All finishes should be non-toxic.

General - No cracked, imperfect or seconds may be exhibited or sold. No findings or raw materials (such as unmounted stones) may be sold. No manufactured or prefabricated objects shall be regarded as acceptable craft work unless the craftsman has transformed it to the extent that its craft character is its dominant feature. Assemblage in any form is not eligible for exhibit unless all units are made by the craftsman.

63. Here's a list of basic standards for craftspeople issued to all entrants by the Washington Square Outdoor Art Exhibit, Inc.

HIGH-HO, WE'RE GOING TO THE FAIR

Well, you've been accepted. Your application, fee, or contract has been received and confirmed. It's a three-day fair — Friday, Saturday, and Sunday, the weather prediction is fine, you're to bring your own tables and chairs, and you'll be responsible for showing and selling. You have from 9:00 to 10:00 the first morning to pull in your van and set up. The show starts at 10:00 a.m. and ends at 5:00 p.m. The fair area is fenced and there are volunteers or hired guards who will look after your work overnight, so you needn't pack it all up each day and unpack the next. Check these details in your application. If you're responsible for safekeeping overnight, you'll have to truck it home each evening or make some other arrangements to guarantee it won't be stolen. Often, even with fences and guards, the fair-runners say they won't be responsible for losses. There are some fair promoters who will guarantee responsibility for lost or stolen items when the fair is held in buildings that can be locked.

Now the fair is a week away and you've been working on the items you want to bring. Rumor is that this will be a good fair — as it has been for the past five years. It's well advertised, and your particular craft has done well there before. Friday and Saturday are good days and your location appears to be excellent — near but not too near the hamburger and ice cream concessions. So you plan to bring $400.00 to $1,000 worth of goods, hoping to sell out.

Tents and Display Structures. Since this particular fair is outdoors, what equipment will you need? You could bring just a folding table and chairs, but there's sun and rain to think about. Should you carry some two-by-fours, nails, hammer, and heavy plastic sheets with you to build a booth? Or should you buy a canopy? What about the fair grounds — are they grass and dirt, or cement? We haven't figured out how to get tent stakes in sidewalks, but sometimes nearby trees or fences help tie some things down. If you have a large enough vehicle or roof rack and plan to go to a number of fairs, a permanent structure of two-by-fours with holes for bolts and nuts (for easy set-up and take-down), plus some roof canvas, are good bets. Such structures when made well, can be set up on sidewalk or flat ground and, if attractive, will draw customers to your stand. The typical space allotment at outdoor fairs is a 10 × 10 foot square. Structures made to fit within this area will be useful for almost all fairs. Where you get more space, the additional area can be used for signs, another outdoor table, or just walk-around space that will be useful when, hopefully, your booth gets crowded with people.

Plastic sheets for roofs and walls can be used to protect your display against sun or light rain. But nothing can save you from a squall or heavy wind and rain. It has a way of creeping in, especially overnight when you're not there to pick a carton off the floor or wrap something in plastic. Once we even managed to get water in our camera lens, not an easy thing to accomplish.

To protect your goods at night, heavy plastic or vinyl sheets tied with nylon rope are best. Also, put any wrapped goods on your tables and off the ground. Cardboard cartons turn into runny paper mud in a good rain and plastic garbage, or "heavy duty" lawn, bags are too thin for the job. As for yourself, dress informally so you won't ruin your clothes if you get drenched. Often, right after a downpour the sun comes out in all its glory and you'll dry out fast. Unfortunately, your crafts will sometimes take days to dry, or they may even be ruined. As for the potters, we love to watch them merely turn over their pots and empty out the water.

Displaying Your Craft. When setting up your booth at a fair, you should make an attractive, eye-catching display. Crowded, messy tables with items piled all over each other don't work. It's better to put a few things out and add more later as they sell. You should also arrange your tables or booth so you can keep an eye on everything without much difficulty. Even if you have two people to watch your booth, one will be leaving at times for a break, so you don't want to have a situation where your back will have to be turned away from a customer. If you have tables with coverings draped to the ground in front, you can keep all your boxes and extra supplies out of sight.

You'll find that certain kinds of displays are useful and attractive for your particular craft. Friends of ours who make stained-glass ornaments use a light box they've constructed themselves. With light shining through these ornaments, this box shows off their best qualities. Another couple who make pottery put shelves between the bars of a child's old swing set and hang planters from the top bar.

Pricing Your Work. In Chapter 2, Pricing, we discussed wholesale and retail prices. At a fair you're selling retail to the general public, but there's more to consider than this. People often expect to spend less for items bought at a fair than those purchased in a store. Your fellow craftspeople may be charging less than their retail prices, which means you should probably lower yours to compete with them. Your prices may vary from fair to fair, depending upon the percentage or fee the promoters take out of your profits. Another thing to consider is the time you spend driving to the fair and sitting there selling your wares. As a general guideline we keep our fair prices at about ¾ of our regular retail prices, except when the promoters take over 20%. In that case we charge full retail prices. Try these guidelines in the beginning. After that you'll learn from experience.

Cash. At most fairs you'll be collecting money from customers and making change. A cash box with separate compartments for bills and change will be useful. Fill it with ten

Sales Tax Guide (7%)

Item	Cost	Tax	Total
Barrette	$ 2.00	$ .14	$ 2.14
Watchband	4.00	.28	4.28
Skinny Belt	5.00	.35	5.35
Wide Belt	9.00	.63	9.63
Small Bag	16.00	1.12	17.12
Medium Bag	19.00	1.33	20.33
Large Bag	24.00	1.68	25.68

64. This sales tax guide is based on 7% tax but you should make one up based on your own prices and local sales tax.

to twenty singles, two or three fives, and plenty of coins. Stuff the box with paper while transporting it so your change doesn't get mixed up.

Any state that has a sales tax requires that you collect it on all retail sales and turn it in periodically to the state government (see Chapter 1). Once you've done so, they'll send you forms and instructions. You may find that your sales tax varies from county to county, as it does in New York State. Whenever you go to a fair, find out what the sales tax percentage is for that county. A chart listing the sales tax for each of your regular prices (see Figure 64) will save time and ensure accuracy when a customer is ready with his money.

For your own records and because you'll have to turn in all taxes collected, keep a tally on all sales (see Figure 65). Take down as much information as you can, especially in the beginning. With a tally sheet properly filled out, at the end of each day you'll know the total sales, total taxes collected, and exactly which items sold. You may find that one design or color outsold all the rest or that one particular item didn't sell at all. After collecting this information for at least the first few fairs you go to you'll be able to tell which products the public is most attracted to.

Sales Slips. Sales pads can be purchased in office-supply stores. They come with carbon paper so you can make an original for the customer and a copy for yourself (see Figure 66). Note that there's a place to put the date, the customer's name, the item sold, the amount, the tax, and the total. There also should be room at the top for you to print or stamp your name, address, and telephone number.

Since fair customers aren't shopping in a store, they don't expect a sales slip or receipt for their purchase. There are advantages to using them, however. With your name and address on the top, the customer can get in touch with you for future purchases. Saving your copy of the sales slip gives you a record of the transaction that you can total up at the end of the day. The tally sheet and business cards will serve both these purposes too, so it's your choice as to which will best serve your needs.

Tools. On many fair applications you'll be asked if you're willing to demonstrate your craft. Demonstrations always attract crowds — they like to watch a craftsperson busy at work. They may not always buy something, but at least you'll have them enthralled. So if you do plan to demonstrate, you'll need a full set of tools and materials for the articles you plan to make. If your work requires an electrical outlet, check with the promoters ahead of time to make sure there will be one available.

Even if you're not going to demonstrate, you may require a few tools. Leather-workers, for example, will often be asked to shorten a belt or change a buckle. If you make jewelry you may have to change an earwire or solder something. In any case, think carefully about the types of repairs or changes you may have to make and make up a list of the necessary tools and materials you'll want to take with you when you go to the fair.

Miscellaneous Items. If the fair you're going to runs into evening hours, consider bringing some floodlights or spotlights. For this, you'll need a screw-in socket, extension cords, reflectors, clamps, and heavy tape. Of course, first make sure there's an electrical outlet available.

When tables and chairs aren't supplied by the fair promoters, bring your own. We've found that 6 × 3 foot folding aluminum tables are excellent. A folding webbed lawn chair is our favorite because it's easily transported, light, and comfortable.

Tablecloths can be attractive, particularly Turkish or Indian prints. But beware of an

Sales Tally Sheet

August 4, 1973
Ithaca Fair

Amount	Item	Price	Tax	Total
1	Barrette, blue flower	$ 2.00	$ .14	$ 2.14
2	Skinny Belts, 1 brown edge, 1 red flower	10.00	.70	10.70
1	Small bag, tan/brown, sunburst	16.00	1.12	17.12
3	Keyrings, all flower, red, blue, burgundy	3.00	.21	3.21
1	Large bag, pussy willow, black	24.00	1.68	25.68
1	Wide belt, Indian center, tan	9.00	.63	9.63
2	Wide belts, flower, red & green	18.00	1.26	19.26
4	Barrettes, 1 yellow flower, 1 brown center, 2 red p.w.	8.00	.56	8.56
Totals		$90.00	$6.30	$96.30

65. *A sales tally sheet is useful for keeping financial records but it will also show you which of your products are selling best.*

HOLY COW LEATHER
180 Horton Road
Newfield, N. Y. 14867
Tel. 564-9022

Aug 4 19*73*

M *Margaret Chase*

Address_____

1	2 skinny belts		
2	1 brown edge		
3	1 red flower	10	00
4	tax		70
5	$	10	70
6			
7			
8			
9			

#29

*66. You may prefer to use sales slips in addition to (or instead of)
the sales tally sheet. Make two copies — one for yourself and one for
the customer.*

interesting phenomenon called capillary action – if part of your tablecloth gets wet from dangling in a puddle, slowly but surely the rest of the cloth will suck up the water and your goods on the cloth will also absorb it. We've moved from burlap to tapestry to vinyl, and until they develop a bug that eats plastic we'll stick to that. At our last fair we encountered a new plague – dust. It was a county fair suitable for car racing, cows, pigs, carnival rides, and tractors, but not for cloth. Our vinyl sponged off easily.

Poster board and thick felt marking pens are also useful, as are Scotch tape and masking tape. Every so often we get the urge to make a sign listing prices or some merits of our product, or perhaps just our name. Posters, tacks, tape, stapling gun, little nails – we've found use for all of them at one time or another.

What else should you bring? Naturally if you're living away from home, bring simple toilet articles and some changes of clothing. But near home or far, here are some other items we've added to our list over the years: mosquito repellent, suntan lotion, soft white hats or other sun-reflecting garments. Picture yourself sitting, standing, and chatting in 90° weather, with or without humidity, and then write up your own list. Bring a food cooler for sandwiches, a thermos for lemonade, etc.

HANDLING CUSTOMERS

From our own experience and that of other craftspeople, how you handle potential customers does make a difference. Some people place more value on it than others, but certainly a smile and a "hello" are the least you can do. Granted, none of us likes to be pestered by a clinging sales clerk, but often a simple, "May I help you?" will clinch the sale.

Keep your eyes and ears open. Some customers are shy and afraid to bother you with their requests, especially if you have your head down and are glued to a book, or are heavily engaged in a conversation with your neighbor. Be attentive to your customers and try to develop a sensitivity to their needs. Some will want to browse for awhile before they make up their mind. But if you see someone pondering over which of two items to buy, you can help him speed up his decision: "Would you like this one?" or, "I think that one looks best on you."

If you want to try some real salesmanship, as soon as a potential customer shows an interest in a particular item, start talking about it. For instance, "That bag you're looking at has been hand carved from real cowhide, you know. And that particular design is one-of-a-kind. When you buy a bag like that, you know it's going to last forever." You may feel your products should "sell themselves," but people often will admire things without buying them. A little sales talk can help make up an undecided mind in your favor.

Wholesale Buyers. Often people that own or work at little shops go to craft fairs to find new suppliers. Don't be surprised if one of them approaches you. If you go to a big fair where wholesale buyers are expected to come, it's a good idea to have wholesale order forms. You can pick these up at an office-supply store.

When a wholesale buyer comes to your booth at a fair, he may expect to buy your products at 50% of what you're selling them for at the fair. This is fine if you're charging full retail prices and are prepared to sell them wholesale. But as we discussed earlier, your fair prices may often be lower than full retail. If you have a printed or mimeographed wholesale price list, hand this to the buyer and explain that these are your wholesale prices. Otherwise simply tell him the wholesale price for each item he's interested in. Don't let him bully you with the argument that he can't sell them in his store for more than your price at the fair. Another alternative of course, if you don't want to sell wholesale, is to refuse the order. We've developed several good wholesale accounts through craft fairs, so if you're interested, this might be an added bonus to your regular fair sales.

A-Sittin' and A-Chattin'. Most fairs leave you with some non-selling time, which is really an understatement. Even at good fairs we may "work," or handle sales, for a combined total of about three or four hours. So there's always time for sitting and chatting or walking around. Plan for it by bringing something to read — few fairs sell your favorite science fiction. Or else, look around at the other exhibits, talk to other craftspeople, get new ideas for your work, buy a frisbee, or find a swimming hole or pool. Just talking with other craftspeople who are a bit different from your buddy at the office can be interesting. Many friendships start at fairs and continue over the years, whether just from one fair to another or socially at home. We have no doubt that part of what draws us to fairs, no matter how bad the last one may have been, is meeting people.

If you're musically inclined, bring along your guitar, harmonica, or whatever you play. It's a pretty sure bet there will be other strings, pipes, or drums at the larger fairs (say, over 80 craftspeople). When you've found the other music people, whether sales wax or wane, and you're strummin', hummin', and singin', you may forget why you came to the fair (or you may find out why you came!).

Of course, you can always work during lulls. You can make new items, or perhaps bring along some partially finished goods that can be easily completed at the fair. People who come to watch may stay to buy.

Another item we bring is a small portable radio. We've never brought or seen a portable television at a fair and never hope to see one — somehow it just doesn't seem fitting and proper. At a fair you live more in the here and now and usually participate in what's going on around you.

We usually bring food and drink, particularly for one day or near-by fairs. There is something about fair food that neither the pocketbook nor the stomach can take much of. We're a captive market, and get hungry just as we do at home, and even thirstier. Since it's hard to get to a supermarket, the people who run the food concessions have us at their mercy. When something is in demand the price frequently goes up, and occasionally the quality goes down. So to save yourself money and a probable stomach-ache, bring a food cooler and thermos.

Living Arrangements. At overnight fairs away from home you'll have to make sleeping arrangements — they can range from your car to a suite at the Ritz. We usually steer for somewhere in the middle. Many fairs are within a short ride of our state and national parks. With some camping equipment and as little as $2.00 you can get a spot for your car and tent with toilet and shower facilities, a barbeque pit, and a beautiful setting. Needless to say, bring your bug repellent. Flashlight, lanterns, matches, a pot of tea, etc., all help pass the time away.

Motels aren't too expensive — $5.00 to $20.00 for two, and nearly all the comforts of home. If you have time, check out motels on the way to the fair or even reserve rooms in advance. Fairs sometimes fill up nearby motels, and after the fair you'll be too tired to check around.

Often the big fair-runners try to find living quarters for the craftspeople. For example, we've enjoyed a dorm in a nearby college. These particular fair-runners even planned activities for our evening pleasure, such as slide shows and discussions, and had a jukebox and beer.

Another place to stay, with a bit of luck, is at a friend's, or with other craftspeople who live in the area. Here you suffer the normal guilt of putting their kids out on the porch, but usually the price is right.

CHECKLIST

1. Send in fair application and fee.

2. Mark fair dates on your calendar.

3. Plan your work schedule to provide enough finished items by fair date.

4. If fair is far from home, arrange for living quarters while away.

5. Plan driving schedule.

6. Pack car or van as much ahead of time as possible.

7. Check off each item on your "to bring" list:

    a. products to sell
    b. price tags
    c. sales slips
    d. money box with plenty of change
    e. bags for people to carry their merchandise away in (paper lunch bags will do)
    f. tents, wood for booth, etc.
    g. tables and chairs
    h. table covering, plastic sheets, etc.
    i. food, drink
    j. warm and cool clothing
    k. tools for your craft
    l. paper, pens, pads, poster boards, felt markers
    m. personal items
    n. things to do — books, radio, etc.
    o. lights, extension cords, etc.
    p. toys to keep children busy
    q. first aid kit
    r. miscellaneous tools — staple gun, hammer, pliers, screwdriver, tape, tacks, wire, string, etc.

8. Mark out your trip on a map, bring map.

9. Leave early enough in case you get lost. Depending on your product and display, it may take a long time for you to set up.

10. High-Ho, you're off to the fair!

11

TRADE
SHOWS

As your business grows you'll probably want to show your goods to a large number of potential buyers at one time. Trade shows are composed of manufacturers, distributors, and sales representatives who get together to show their merchandise to a large group of buyers. Usually the show is restricted to certain products. For example, there are apparel shows, gift shows, leather goods shows, boutique shows, shoe shows, etc. There are regional trade shows that take place throughout the country, such as in Dallas, Buffalo, Chicago, and Washington, D.C. The national shows usually take place in New York City or sometimes in Los Angeles. There are also international shows taking place in New York City, as well as in foreign countries throughout the world.

WHY GO TO A TRADE SHOW?

There are two basic reasons for going to a trade show — to increase your wholesale business if you sell wholesale, or if you have a retail store, to find new items to purchase for your shop. If you're going to buy for a retail store, you'll be admitted free, in fact solicited, to go to trade shows. In this chapter we'll be talking mostly about going to a trade show as a manufacturer in order to increase wholesale sales.

There are a lot of side benefits to be gained from attending trade shows. You'll see first hand what your competition is doing. You may be able to make some good contacts with jobbers (see Chapter 13) and sales representatives who want to handle your line. You also may run into some new suppliers. They come to the show because they expect to see manufacturers who might use their products.

Finding Out About Trade Shows. Ask the buyers you sell to what trade shows they attend and whether they think it will be worth your while to attend. Some will be more than happy to share this information with you.

Another way to find out about trade shows is to subscribe to trade magazines. A trade magazine is published specifically for people doing business in a particular trade. For example, the trade magazine *Handbags and Accessories* is bought by retailers, manufacturers, and suppliers. These magazines run stories on retail shops, new styles in their field, new types of materials, people in the business, laws affecting the business, etc. Manufacturers advertise their products, and suppliers of raw materials sometimes adver tise in them. Ads are also exchanged between manufacturers looking for sales reps and vice versa.

If you sell to craft and gift shops, *Gifts and Decorative Accessories* would be the trade magazine to subscribe to. It lists all the gift shows plus others throughout the country. For any craft pertaining to apparel or accessories, such as jewelry, belts, handbags, cloth-ing, or hats, *Womens Wear Daily* is a must. It comes out daily, but you can get a once-a-week subscription that covers your specialty. You'll find out about all the related trade shows, and also find ads for and by representatives, help wanted, closeouts offered to businesses, fashion trends, used machines, etc.

We also subscribe to *Leather and Shoes, Boutique,* and *Handbags and Accessories*. They're not always fantastically rich in information, but we usually get a useful tidbit from each of them and sometimes one little piece of information can be worth a whole lot. Refer to the appendix for the addresses of these trade magazines.

SELECTING TRADE SHOWS

It's important to choose the correct trade show for your craft. For example, we started off by going to several gift shows. Then we tried the International Leather Goods Show and the National Boutique Show. The results indicated that the gift show was wrong for us, but the leather goods and boutique shows were right. We still plan to try several other types of shows, such as the shoe show, the mail order show, and the premium show.

Basically, you want to find a show that attracts the kind of buyers who normally buy your products. If you sell your craft only to gift shops and galleries, the various gift shows would probably be best for you. If you make any kind of jewelry, you have more variety to choose from. The gift show, the boutique show, and perhaps even an apparel show might be good for you. We saw candles at the boutique show and the gift shows. We've seen all kinds of leather at the leather show, the boutique show, and the shoe show.

Regional or National Shows? Whether to go to regional or national shows depends on where you live and how much money you have to spend. The regional shows usually cost less than national or international shows, but the turnout is smaller too. If you live near New York City we recommend national shows. Other good shows are in the major cities of the country — Dallas, Chicago, Los Angeles, etc. We went to two regional shows in Rochester and Syracuse, New York, that were pretty bad. The reason may also have been, however, that these were gift shows.

Space at these shows is rented by booth, with the average small size being 8 X 10 feet or 10 X 10 feet. The fees start at around $150.00 but can run as high as $1,000 for a small booth at a big national show. Sometimes there is a waiting list and you can't even get into a show. For example, the National Gift Show is held at the Coliseum in New York with the overflow housed at the Sheraton. You may have to go to the Sheraton for a few years before you are able to "move up" to the Coliseum. Naturally all the best spots at these shows are already taken by regular customers. When a show is held at a hotel, some exhibitors and salespeople take rooms at the hotel.

You might want to try a regional show if it's your first one so you'll get the feel of it. In fact, if time allows, why not first attend one as a visitor to see what it's like? Write to the people running the show and ask if you can have a visitor's badge because you're considering entering the show the next time it's held. Then you'll be able to see if your type of merchandise is exhibited, what kinds of buyers attend, how busy the show is, etc.

Mail Order, Premium, and Variety Shows. The buyer who comes to a mail order show is looking for merchandise to sell through the mail. Buyers include Sears Roebuck, Speigel, J.C. Penney, Spencer Gifts, etc. This is the type of show where you go to make initial contacts. Don't expect to write up a lot of actual orders at the show. These buyers will want your absolute rock-bottom price, and they'll be buying in large volume, if at all.

Premiums are merchandise that's given away or sold at a reduced price in order to persuade a customer to buy a company's product. For example, the free ring in a cereal box or the set of bowls you can send away for for $2.00 and a box top are premiums. If you have a product that could be used as a premium, it might be worth your while to attend this show. Again, the buyers will be looking for low prices, volume orders, quick delivery, etc.

The variety merchandise shows draw buyers from big department stores and chain stores. As the name indicates, there's a variety of merchandise displayed, such as shoes, jewelry, and apparel. Here again they'll be interested in low price, volume orders, quick delivery, reliability, etc. You may find it best to visit these shows first before actually exhibiting. Talk to other exhibitors to get some tips on what the buyers are looking for.

Additional Costs. Besides the show fee, you can run up many additional costs. For example, there's usually a decorator service and delivery service available. The delivery service brings your merchandise to your booth and the decorator service decorates your booth for you. Basic services that come with your booth are usually no more than a sign with your name on it, perhaps a couple of tables and risers (wooden shelves), and *perhaps* some sheets for covering. You must provide or pay for everything else. At the National Boutique Show only union labor was allowed to do any work at the show (stapling material to tables, painting a sign, etc.). In other words, you had to pay workmen $15.00 to $25.00 per hour rather than do it yourself.

You also have to eat, drink, and sleep for the three or four days of the show, plus the extra day it takes to set your booth up. You can bet that the food sold at the show is going to be extra expensive, especially in the large cities. Unless you live close enough to drive back and forth each day, you'll need to rent a room in a motel or hotel. Then there are taxis, subway and bus fares, tolls, tips, etc. All in all, make sure you have plenty of extra money with you for show expenses. Such expenses, of course, are necessary to do business and can be considered as such at tax time (see Chapter 17).

SETTING UP YOUR BOOTH

The show-runners set aside certain days ahead of time for you to set up your booth. We find that one day in advance is usually plenty. Basically, you want to set up the most attractive booth possible, one that will attract the attention of passersby. This is most important for a new business. If you were well established, buyers would be looking for you. But since you're not, you want to make them stop at your booth rather than continuing down the aisle to an old favorite. There are many exhibitors at these shows —

the National Boutique Show had 10 floors of the McAlpin Hotel filled — making it difficult for a buyer to get to see every booth. By the middle of the first day they're tired, their feet hurt, and everything is beginning to look the same to them. This is what you're up against.

Your exact method of display will of course depend on your craft. But in general, you need something at eye level to attract the crowd. Use contrasting colors and shapes, build up your display as high as possible, and have something right out front that people can examine closely. If you can think of a good gimmick, such as a giveaway, use it. One leather company we've seen gives away a free key ring to every buyer who stops at their booth. If you have a small, inexpensive item you can afford to give away, try it.

When you go to a show, study every one of your competitors closely. What types of display do they use? What kinds of racks or stands do they have? What types of background materials do they use? What kind of catalogs and price sheets do they have? Keep looking for new ideas and trying to improve what you've got.

What to Bring. Bring enough of your best samples to make an attractive display. You may want to bring extra because samples are often swapped or sold at the end of a show. If the show management doesn't provide tables or table coverings, you'll need to bring these. If you plan to use pegboard, metal racks, or stands, bring some. (Tables, chairs, racks, etc., can usually be rented at the show if you prefer.)

Include extra literature — price sheets, business cards, order forms, etc. Other handy items are Scotch tape, masking tape, paper clips, stapler, staple gun, tacks, string, scratch pads, pens, pencils, pocket calculator, pliers, scissors, ruler or tape measure, envelopes, stamps, manilla folders, hooks, and traveler's checks (better than a lot of loose cash).

Advertising. There's usually a booklet printed listing all the exhibitors alphabetically, by booth numbers, and by product. This listing is included as part of your booth fee. If you want additional ads in the book, it costs extra. You'll be given information on these ads when signing up for the show.

In addition, you may wish to advertise in the trade magazine related to the show. For example, if you're going to be in a gift show, you may want to take an ad out in *Gifts and Decorative Accessories* for the issue just before the show. As yet, we haven't done any of this advertising, mainly because we can't afford it. When we can, we hope to try some small ads in the *Boutique* or *Handbags and Accessories* magazines.

To help advertise the trade show itself, the management of the show will supply you with free envelope stuffers, stickers, or other advertising material for you to send to all your customers reminding them that you'll be exhibiting in the show. Send these out well in advance to any of your customers who might be able to attend the show.

WHAT TO EXPECT

Immediate results aren't always fantastic, especially for new exhibitors. We've exhibited at four different trade shows to date. Our actual sales written at the show vary from one order to twenty orders, or from $100.00 to $1,300. At a leather show last year, however, we made our first contact with a customer who ended up giving us $10,000 worth of orders by the end of the year. At the Boutique Show we handed out a lot of literature. By the second week after we returned, we had received two more telephone orders from people who had taken literature at the show. We're still expecting future results from contacts made there.

For these reasons it's difficult to evaluate the exact monetary value of a particular trade show. Naturally you want to write up as many actual orders at the show as possible. If you do write up $10,000 worth of orders, you don't have to worry about the value of the show — you *know* it was great. But don't be disappointed if this doesn't happen. It may take months to finalize sales initiated at the show. It's difficult also to put a price on the value of a new customer who stays with you for the next ten years.

We've heard that many buyers won't buy from you the first time they see you at a show because they want to see if you're still in business by the next show. Then they'll confidently place an order with you. So don't give up on a show after one time.

Follow-Up. When you come back from the show your brief case will undoubtedly be filled with names and addresses, business cards, etc., of people you met — suppliers, sales representatives, jobbers, and retail stores. Some will want more information and others, such as suppliers, may have left you literature and other information. Sort through all of these and send letters or literature, where necessary.

Process all the orders you took immediately. That is, check the credit references and ratings of each account. We usually state right at the show that we'll ship C.O.D. unless the store has a Dun and Bradstreet rating or can give us three references. Most of them are honest enough at the show to tell us to ship C.O.D. if they don't have an established credit rating. If, however, we find after our credit check that we can't ship a particular store on credit, we send a letter asking if we may ship the order C.O.D.

After the show, most trade show managers will provide you with a listing of every buyer who attended the show. You may want to use this as a mailing list to send future literature and prices on new products. If you find that this list is too general, try asking every buyer who stops at your booth to list his name with you so you can send him literature. Or, look at each buyer's name tag when he comes into your booth and jot it down after he leaves. Then you can check out his address later.

CONCLUSION

If you want to build up your wholesale business, see what your competition is doing, meet sales reps, jobbers, and suppliers in your field, trade shows are the places to go. They take money and time, but can prove to be invaluable to you. Check out the various types of trade shows, visit a couple first if you prefer, and then sign up for the one you think might be best for you.

CHECKLIST

1. A trade show is a place where manufacturers, distributors, and sales reps get together to show their merchandise to wholesale buyers.

2. If you have a retail store go to trade shows to see new merchandise, compare values, and order for your shop.

3. As a manufacturer, go to increase your wholesale sales, see your competition, and make contacts.

4. Pick a trade show that fits your craft, such as a gift show if you sell mostly to gift shops.

5. Find out about trade shows by asking buyers at stores you now sell to, and by reading trade magazines.

6. Costs for booth fees can run from $150.00 to $1,000, with national shows costing more than regional shows.

7. Additional costs are delivery and decorator fees, food, drink, lodging, tips, travel, etc.

8. Plan your booth set-up with care so it's as attractive as possible.

9. Bring samples, table coverings, literature, price lists, order forms, Scotch tape, masking tape, paper clips, stapler, staple gun, tacks, string, scratch pads, pens, pencils, pocket calculator, pliers, scissors, ruler or tape measure, envelopes, stamps, manilla folders, hooks, traveler's checks.

10. Your name will automatically be listed in the trade show guidebook handed out to each buyer at the beginning of the show. Additional advertising in the guidebook or trade magazines costs extra.

11. Results can vary widely. But a show can't be accurately evaluated strictly by orders written up while there. Contacts made, information received, number of years new customers stay with you, future orders made from original contacts, etc., are all part of the show results.

12. Follow-up on orders and leads after you return from a show.

12

RETAIL
STORES

In this chapter we'll briefly discuss the planning, operation, and problems of a retail store. If you watch your town or city carefully, you'll notice that many new stores open and then after a short period close down. Why do they close and what makes the successful ones stay in business? How can you make sure your store will survive? These are the questions we'll try to answer in this chapter.

OPENING A STORE

The smaller your town or city, the more general and varied your merchandise will have to be. For example, in New York City you'll find an entire shop for nearly every item you can think of — a kite shop, a stamp shop, etc. But in a small town a kite shop couldn't find enough customers to keep it in business. So first of all consider the size of the town or locality where you plan to open your shop.

If you make one particular craft, such as silver jewelry, consider opening a shop in partnership with several other craftspeople. This will give your shop variety. Another idea is to sell the crafts of other people on consignment. Having a general crafts shop, gift shop, or gallery, might offer ways to reach a larger clientele.

If you live in a big city or if there's a demand for your particular craft, then you have no problem. For example, some friends opened up a leather shop in Berkeley, California, and between the tourist traffic and nearby college students, they've had plenty of business.

Potential Customers and Location. Who are your potential customers? In what section of the town or city do they live and what shopping areas do they frequent? You should set up your store as close as possible to your clientele. If your craft appeals mostly to college students, open a shop in a campus shopping area. If most of your potential customers prefer a particular shopping mall, this is where you should be.

Choose the absolutely top location for your store, even if it means higher rent. Any savings in rent won't make up for the loss of profits you'll have because you chose a second-best or third-best location. We know — we opened a shop in a third-best location in order to save rent, and we found out fast that it wasn't worth it.

So before you sign the lease, make certain you've checked it out carefully. Ask people in the area 'where they shop the most. Stand around on a weekday and watch the pedestrian traffic that walks up and down the block and goes in and out of the store you're considering. Then do the same on a Saturday. Remember, there's no point in putting all the work, time, and money into a store if you start out in the wrong location.

Competition. If no one has ever had a store similar to the one you're considering in your neighborhood, it doesn't necessarily mean the store won't be successful. It could be that no one has ever thought of the idea and now the time is just ripe. On the other hand, maybe there are good reasons, such as not enough interest, for such a store existing.

If there have been similar stores that have failed in the past, you'd better check out why. In Ithaca, New York, for example, several leather shops had tried in the past, but none lasted more than a year or two. Should this have indicated to us that Ithaca wasn't a good place for a leather shop? Perhaps. There are some 20,000 college students in the area, but very few tourists compared to Berkeley, California.

If there are one or two stores in operation that have a similar format to the one you're planning, it doesn't mean you shouldn't open another one. At least you know that the town or neighborhood can support that kind of store. The question is, can it support another one? How can you make yours more attractive than your competitor's? Can you get a better location, advertise it better, or even give the same quality for less?

Capital. Don't try to open a store on a shoestring. First, you'll probably have to sign at least a year's lease, if not longer. Next, there are remodeling costs, electricity, telephone, fixtures (lights, display racks and cases, etc.), and insurance. This is just to get the bare, empty store in operation.

Next, even if you make all your own merchandise, you'll need enough of it to stock the store fully. If you buy any merchandise — and a need for variety often demands this — it will have to be purchased in advance. Even if you're able to get it on credit, you'll only have a month's breathing space. Buying on consignment might help, but make certain you're dealing with reliable craftspeople who will have the goods ready by opening day and not remove them three days later for a local craft fair (see Chapter 9 for consignment agreements).

Now that your store is clean, well-lit, stocked, and insured, you're ready to open the doors. But who knows you're opening? If you don't advertise, no one will. Advertising can be a big part of your costs.

And last, who's going to operate your store six or seven days a week, and one or more nights? Are you going to do it all yourself? It's going to be pretty rough if you try, so undoubtedly you'll need some help. This means money for salaries, payroll taxes, workmen's compensation, etc.

We want to emphasize that you shouldn't try to start a store without capital. If you have a few thousand of your own, you may be able to get a bank or Small Business Association Loan (see Chapter 14) for the rest, but whatever way you get it, you *will* need money.

Display. The way your store looks to people, both from the outside and on the inside, is very important. From the outside, you want to attract people as they walk down the street so they'll look in your window and walk in the door. To do this you'll need a sign with your name on it — something attractive and visible, preferably sticking out perpendicular to the store front so it catches people's eye from a distance. The second part of the attraction is to have a good window display. Use your creativity to come up with interesting displays that let the customer know what kind of merchandise he's likely to find inside your store. Change the display often enough so regular customers will want to keep looking to see what's new. Study window displays in other stores to get ideas.

Now that you've got the customer walking in your door, you want to make him glad he did, you want to make him feel free to browse around, ask questions, and finally find something he wants to buy. The fact that you may be selling a handcrafted item doesn't mean your store should look like a disorganized mess. You can use any display theme you wish, and a rustic one is fine with crafts, but the basic ingredients of good display are still important. Your store should be clean. The initial impact when walking into it should be pleasant, inviting, and colorful. All merchandise should be visible, easy to look at, with prices clearly marked. Merchandise should be displayed to set off its best aspects. For example, a box of items thrown together for people to rummage through is *not* very inviting. You don't want your store to look too crowded, nor too empty. Some merchandise lends itself to particular types of displays. There are belt racks for belts, earring racks for earrings, jewelry cases for jewelry, etc. But use your imagination to come up with new and different displays that will attract the eye.

DEALING WITH CUSTOMERS

Salesmanship is very important in a retail store, just as it is at craft fairs, fleamarkets, or any other direct selling situation. If you jump on every customer with a fast sales pitch that doesn't let up until they leave, you'll lose customers. On the other hand, a customer shouldn't be afraid to ask a question, or feel like he's "bothering" you because you're aloof or absorbed in something else. What you need is to develop a sensitivity to the customer, to know when to ask if he needs help, when to stand back and let him browse, when to suggest, etc. This sensitivity can be developed with practice.

In the beginning try being pleasant when the customer walks in. Smile and say hello. If he stands there uncertainly for a moment, ask if you may help him. If he seems to know exactly what he's looking for and walks toward it, leave him alone for a few minutes. There's no harm in asking a customer if he would like some help. If he says no, you can leave him alone.

Be alert when customers are in the store. Don't read a book or eat your lunch. Always look ready to help and be ready to help. If a customer walks toward the cash register with an article in his hand say, "Would you like to take that?" or, "May I ring that up for you?"

If you're operating the type of store where you work at the craft right in the store, you can modify these rules somewhat. The customer will enjoy watching you make a belt, silver earrings, or whatever, right in front of him. But you shouldn't get so involved that you forget the customer, especially if you're the only one in the store at the time. Taking care of the customer properly should come first. After all, you opened a store to make sales, didn't you?

CASH, CHECKS, AND CREDIT CARDS

When you make each sale, write up a sales receipt (see Figure 67). If your cash register makes a tape receipt, however, this isn't necessary. Put the sales slip or tape receipt from the register in the customer's package. At the end of the day all but a specified amount of money, say $50.00, should be removed from the register. This cash should be matched against the register total or sales slip copies to see that no errors were made. Then the money should be deposited in the bank. By the way, you might consider taking money to the bank at different times of the day or week. Vary your routine so that you're not known to have $100.00 or $1,000 on you every night at 6:00 p.m.

If you take checks, stamp the back of each one immediately with your bank deposit stamp (ask you bank for such a rubber stamp if you don't already have one). This way if the store is robbed, the thief won't be able to cash these checks (see Chapter 5 for precautions against bad checks).

For a small percentage of sales you can allow your customers to use Bank Americard or Master Charge credit cards. See your local banks to find out how these work. After all, many people will buy things on a credit card that they'd otherwise do without if they had to pay cash.

Advertising. No matter how great a location you have, you'll probably still find it advantageous to advertise. You want as many people as possible to know you're there, what kinds of things you sell, how good your prices are, when you're having a sale, or when you get in something new. You especially want to reach the people who would buy your type of merchandise if they knew about you.

It's difficult to say exactly how much you should spend on advertising and where you should advertise. In general, retail stores spend between 3% and 10% of total sales on advertising. I'm sure there are some that don't spend any, but I wonder how long they last and what sales potential they're missing out on.

We have used radio and newspaper advertising. Since our product appeals to young people, especially college students, we advertised weekly in the two college newspapers in our town. Many people have come into the store saying they heard or saw our ad. Figure 68 shows examples of several ads we've used in the past.

As far as costs go, radio is much more expensive than newspapers. Also, the smaller the station or paper, the less expensive it will be. We tried two radio stations — one listened to by teenagers and one by college students. We try to advertise special sales or new items.

Look at the newspapers in your area and notice who advertises in them. Listen to the various radio stations. Then try a few and see what the results are.

Protection. Theft can be a serious problem. It's becoming so common that some stores automatically add 5% or 10% to their prices to cover theft losses. There are all kinds of ingenious systems, including closed circuit television, to help owners catch or discourage thieves. But a small store usually can't afford these systems. So what are you going to do about it?

Don't think it won't happen to you. Just because you're small, make handcrafted items, and are "one of the group," don't think people won't steal. There's someone out there who will steal from anyone if he thinks he can get away with it.

First we suggest you keep an accurate inventory of all goods in your store so you'll at

HOLY COW LEATHER
180 Horton Road
Newfield, N. Y. 14867
Tel. 564-9022

Sold By_____ Date __2/25__ 19___

Name_____

Address_____

		REG. NO. / AMT. REC'D	ACCT. FWD.	
1	1	wide belt	8	00
1	2	skinny belt	4	00
2	3	Keyrings @ 1.00	2	00
	4		14	00
	5			
	6	TAX		98
	7		14	98
	8			
	9			
	10			
	11			
	12			
	13	**17**		
	14			

5A20 Rediform

67. *This shows how a sales receipt should be written up. A copy should be given to the customer and a copy kept for your records.*

68. These are newspaper ads we've used in the past.

least know if you've lost something (see Chapter 3, on inventory systems). Next we suggest you set up your store so that all the merchandise is visible, that is, so you can keep an eye on it, as well as on customers, at all times. Keep small, expensive items in glass cases where the customer can't pocket them. Position someone near the door so a thief can be spotted and stopped. Sample items may be nailed, stapled, or tied down to a display table.

If your inventory records show you're experiencing a substantial amount of theft, consider some of the anti-theft systems on the market. In some towns store owners are joining together to try to discourage shoplifting. If there's such an organization in your area, join it. If not, maybe you can start one. In any case, stolen goods will come directly out of your profits, so make sure you know what's going on and take steps to remedy it.

Seasons. For most retail stores, Christmas will be the peak season. If you're in a resort area in New England, summer will be a good season. If you're in a resort area in Florida, winter may be best. If you make hammocks or lawn furniture, the warmer the weather the better. In any case, whatever your craft or location, you'll definitely have some good seasons and some bad seasons. The important thing is to be ready for them.

Once you find out what your peak seasons are, you've got to be ready. Your store should be stocked to the hilt. You may need extra sales help at these times. You may wish to advertise more heavily and stay open later. So, you can expect to lay out more money in merchandise and help, put in more time and hard work, but also make more sales and thereby profit.

The peak seasons are great. It's the bad times inbetween that hurt. The trick is to save the money you make during peak times to carry you through the bleak times. Don't figure you can go to Bermuda for a month after a great Christmas, then come home to a lousy February and March, and have to borrow money to make the rent payments. See yourself through a full year first to discover what the trends are.

CONCLUSION

Retail stores have provided nice incomes for one or two families and have even sent the kids to college — but not in the first year. It takes time for the community or neighborhood to get to know you, to think of you whenever they want a gift or your kind of merchandise. Buyers like to check out a new store for awhile. They like to feel comfortable in your place. Part of their good feeling comes from seeing you month in and month out, and knowing your goods are reliable and admired by their friends. This takes time. Occasionally you'll see a thriving store in a location that's not particularly conducive to traffic, but usually it's been there for years and has developed a loyal following who will shop there despite the off-the-beaten-track location.

Your best bet is to find a prime location, have sufficient capital to fix it up attractively, hang in through seasonal slumps, advertise, and present a cheerful, good feeling to the potential buyer. If you do all this, and stick with it, chances are you'll eventually be able to live nicely off the store and perhaps give a thought to a second one someday in another town.

CHECKLIST

1. Decide what type of store you'll open.

2. Choose the best location in your town for your merchandise.

3. Consider the competition.

4. Make sure you have enough capital to cover lease, remodeling, utilities, fixtures, insurance, stock, help, etc.

5. Develop attractive displays, signs, window displays, etc.

6. Develop your salesmanship, and see that your employees do also.

7. Start out each day with the same amount of cash in the register. Deposit excess cash daily in the bank (but not at the same time every day).

8. Rubber-stamp checks immediately with your bank deposit number in case of theft.

9. See your local banks about using Bank Americard and Master Charge. For a small percentage of sales you may increase your volume.

10. Check out advertising rates, audiences, etc., of local newspapers and radio stations. Plan your advertising budget, write some copy, and try it.

11. Keep a running inventory of all merchandise in your store. If any theft is noticed, take action against it. Keep alert.

12. Expect peaks and valleys, or seasonal sales. Get extra stock in for the peak seasons and save your money to tide you over the bleak ones.

13. Be patient. A retail store doesn't always get off the ground in its first year of operation. Work at it, stick with it, and eventually, chances are you'll make it.

13

SALES
REPRESENTATIVES

A sales or manufacturers' representative is a person who sells for a living. He or she usually represents the lines of several manufacturers and covers shops in one or more states. They generally work on a commission basis only, sometimes with expenses paid also. A good sales representative makes a good living. He has to hustle because it's all up to him — the more he sells, the more he makes. Therefore he's always looking for new and better lines that will increase his sales.

DO YOU NEED SALES REPS?

When we first started wholesaling, we went out on the road ourselves, covering stores within a 100-mile radius from us. On vacation trips or visiting relatives, we'd take time out to sell in those cities too. But all in all we found it difficult to cover as much territory as we'd have liked to. Trying to run the production, packing, bookkeeping, and other ends of the business didn't leave us much time for selling, especially on overnight trips.

So one day we said, "Why just sell our goods in the small area where we live? Why not sell to stores all across the country and increase our wholesale business?" This meant part of our profit would go to pay sales commissions, but if it increased over-all sales, we felt it would be worth it.

Basically, if you want to increase your wholesale business or free yourself from selling duties, and can afford a commission percentage in your pricing, you should consider sales reps. If you're afraid of growing too fast, hire one or two at a time. Let your production capacity grow in stages.

Finding Sales Reps. Even though sales reps may represent from two to ten different lines, the lines are usually related. In other words if a rep calls on gift shops and jewelry stores, he'll represent items such as jewelry, china, pottery, and silver. He may represent three different jewelry manufacturers or he may combine general gift items with jewelry. But he certainly isn't going to represent a shoe manufacturer at the same time. Reps pick certain areas of related products so they can sell to similar stores. For example, one of our reps sells a hosiery line to shoe stores and clothing shops. He can carry our handbags and belts because he can sell these items in these stores, too.

So, first decide what type of stores you want your rep to call on and what sort of compatible merchandise he should carry. If gift shops are your main thing, advertise for a rep in *Gifts and Decorative Accessories*. If your craft has anything to do with women's apparel or accessories, advertise in *Womens Wear Daily* (see Figure 69).

Another place to find reps is at trade shows (see Chapter 11). We've seen some exhibitors put small signs up in their booth letting people know they're looking for sales reps. Sometimes a rep who's looking for new lines will come up to you at a show and ask if you're looking for reps in his area. Once a rep called us because he saw our line in one of his stores. The buyer recommended our line to him and eventually a deal was worked out.

What to Offer a Rep. We were quite naïve when we started. At the first trade show we attended we asked several sales reps what the going commission rate was. We got answers from 10% to 20%. We thought a good commission rate would attract reps, so we started to offer 15%. We quickly learned, however, that the going rate in our line of goods was 10%. Some of the big manufacturers of shoes, clothing, etc., offer only 5% to 8%. A jewelry manufacturer we know offers 15%. So it really varies according to the type of merchandise you're offering. In general, the bigger the volume that can be expected on a line, the less the percentage rate. This makes sense — a rep doesn't mind making 5% on a line if he can sell $600,000 a year.

Ask other craftspeople and manufacturers who make a product similar to yours. What do they offer sales reps? Look in Help Wanted under "Sales" in the trade magazines. Sometimes the commission rate is listed right in the ad. Also figure out what you can afford to give in commissions and still make a profit with a competitively priced item.

Types of Agreements. Most sales reps want an exclusive territory. For example, if they cover the states of Pennsylvania and Ohio, they want commissions on all orders received from these two states and they want to be the only sales rep you have in these states. This means you can't hire another rep for the same territory. It also means that you must give your rep commissions on orders that come directly in the mail, through trade shows, etc., from these states aside from the ones the rep sends you directly.

There are modified versions of this agreement. For example, you may have one rep

---

Reps wanted for highly competitive line of latigo
handbags, belts and small accessories. Several
territories open. If you are active, aggressive,
calling on the youth market -- boutiques, specialty,
chain, and department stores, contact Holy Cow
Leather, 180 Horton Rd., Newfield, N.Y. 14867.

---

69. We use this type of ad to attract sales reps.

who calls only on chains and department stores, and another who calls only on little boutique and gift shops. These two reps could probably coexist in the same territory because they don't sell to the same buyers. Another change you might want to make in the basic agreement is that any first-time orders you get at a national trade show will not be commissioned to the rep. He can get commissions on future orders when he follows up.

The important thing is to honor any agreement you make with a sales rep. Some will want all these things spelled out in a written agreement. Others will be looser about it. In general, you'll want to cooperate with a good sales rep who's doing a lot of business for you. A bad one isn't worth keeping.

Showrooms. Some sales reps have showrooms where the merchandise they represent is permanently displayed and there's always someone there to take a customer's order. New York City is the big marketplace. Every decent-size manufacturer has a New York showroom where buyers can go "to market." Other big cities, such as Los Angeles, Boston, and Chicago, also have them.

There are many variations on the way showrooms work. You could establish your own showroom, pay rent and help, etc., but this would be quite expensive. Another way is to offer a rep with a showroom an additional percentage commission, such as 5%. Or else, share expenses with other craftspeople or manufacturers. Problems arise when a Pennsylvania shop comes to the New York showroom and places an order. Who gets the commission, your New York showroom rep or your Pennsylvania rep? It depends on the policy you set up to start with. You could split the commission and give each half. You could give the New York rep the whole commission on that order, with the Pennsylvania rep getting future commissions on follow-up orders. Some of our reps have showrooms and simply get the same commission on products sold there as they would on the road, however these are not New York City showrooms. Before you offer a lot, you should get out there and look at the showroom. If you're paying partial costs or additional commissions, make sure your product is displayed and pushed along with the other lines.

Jobbers. In your search for sales reps you may come across some jobbers. A jobber is someone who buys goods in volume from a manufacturer and resells them wholesale. In general he can get them at a better price because of the volume he buys. Then he resells to retail stores, etc., who buy in smaller quantities.

A jobber, therefore, will want your goods at lower prices than your lowest wholesale price, because he has to go out and sell them wholesale himself. If you feel it's worth it to you to lower your prices that much in order to sell in large volume, then you might consider selling to jobbers. But you may find, especially with handcrafted goods, that the price he demands is just too low and you can't profitably meet it. In that case, don't deal with jobbers.

CLOSING THE DEAL WITH A REP

After you've placed an ad in the trade magazine you'll start to get replies from interested reps. Some give you a lot of information about themselves in their first letter, others say hardly anything at all. They want to know what you have to offer first. To move this glimmer of interest into a closing deal there are several steps to take.

First, send him literature, price lists, photos, etc., to give a complete picture of what you make, what it looks like, and how much it costs. The rep will also be interested in how fast you deliver, what your terms are (net 30 days, etc.), if you have lower volume prices for big orders, when you pay commissions, if you advertise, and if you'll contribute for showroom or trade show costs.

Second, you need to know as much about the rep as possible. Ask for at least three references, preferably from other manufacturers he represents or has represented in the past. If you subscribe to a credit bureau, send for a report on him. Ask him about the kinds of stores he sells to (which ones), how many other lines he carries and what type of merchandise they make. You don't want a rep who is handling your competitor's line also, who has so many lines he won't be able to devote the necessary time to yours, or who goes to the wrong types of stores.

When to Pay Commissions. We pay commissions monthly on shipped orders. For example, if a rep sends in an order at the end of September and we ship it in October, he'll get the commission for it by November 10th (see Figure 70). The dates listed are the dates when the orders were shipped. At the end of the month we add up all shipped orders and a check is sent out before the 10th of the following month.

Don't pay commissions immediately upon receiving the order. Make sure the order is shipped and accepted by the store first. If you try to make a sales rep wait until the customer pays for the order, however, he'll be pretty unhappy. For example, the order received in September, and shipped in October, may not be paid for until November or December, or later if the account is slow. The most standard procedure is to pay after the order has been shipped (see Figure 71).

Confirming Orders. When writing to prospective sales reps, tell them when commissions will be paid. Tell them also that confirming orders will be sent to each store as soon as the order is received by you. To do this, simply get a set of invoices with an extra copy. Type it up (as shown in Chapter 4), and leave the shipping date blank. Then pull out the copy you'll use for the confirming order. Have a rubber stamp made saying "Confirming Order" in large letters and stamp this on the invoice. Write in the expected shipping date and send this copy to the customer. This way they can check to see if the order is correct. It also lets them know you're working on it and do plan to ship on time.

Why Be So Careful? We've had the classic experience illustrating why precautions such as references for sales reps, confirming orders, and paying commissions after an order is shipped, are necessary. In response to the first ad we placed for a sales rep was a phone call from a wonderful gentleman who wanted to handle the line in New England. He said he had two other sales reps working with him and that he thought they could do a great job. His only worry was that *they* had gotten stung by some other leather people in the past and had never received the commissions they were entitled to for sales they had made. Therefore he was a little wary, but willing to give us a chance if we would send commissions out *weekly* as we received orders from him.

He was such a nice-sounding chap, very fatherly, giving us bits of information and advice, that we sent him two complete sets of samples (free of charge) for himself and his men, and sat back and waited for the results. Well, was he fantastic! The first week he sent in $3,000 worth of orders. We were going out of our minds, especially since our capacity was about $500.00 a week production at that time. Each week it continued, more and more orders. We were so thrilled we gladly sent him his commissions at the end of each week.

Smith, Joe   Commissions

	Ship. Date	Account	Order #	Amount	Comm.	Payment	Bal	
1	1.4	Bittertree	Phone	650				1
2	1.5	Clothes tree	letter	2400				2
3	1.5	Town + Country	12/30	3600				3
4	1.18	Unzell's	1/8	6300				4
5	1.23	Carey's	1/7	23300				5
6	1.24	Lynn's Clothing	1/10	5800				6
7	1.29	The Cottage	1/7	11600				7
8	1.29	Peaches + Cream	1/7	23000				8
9	1.29	Children's Clothes	1/14	3600				9
10				80250	8025	8035	0	10
11	2.4	Four Seasons	1/21	1200				11
12		Hamilton Dry Goods	1/22	8700				12
13	2.11	Russell's	2/11	13400				13
14	2.12	Barbara's	2/12	8700				14
15	2.14	Ruth Green's	2/14	6325				15
16								16
17								17
18								18
19								19
20								20
21								21
22								22
23								23
24								24
25								25
26								26
27								27
28								28
29								29
30								30
31								31
32								32
33								33
34								34
35								35
36								36
37								37
38								38
39								39
40								40

70. *This page from our commission record book shows how we record sales reps' commissions by date of shipment.*

12/4	Adlers	$	30.00
12/3	Smiths Dept. Store		100.50
12/3	Morelands Dry Goods		66.50
12/3	The Clothes Tree		56.00
12/4	Burns Dress Shop		103.50
12/6	Mr. B's Apparel		97.00
12/6	Town & Casual		285.00
12/5	C & A Shoes		92.00
12/5	Freidas Fashions		91.50
12/5	Smartee Shoppe		239.00
12/10	Perrens		137.00
12/10	Arthur Mitchel		297.00
12/10	Hearns Dry Goods		54.00
12/11	Athens Colonial		27.00
12/11	Carls Shoes		78.00
12/11	Rheas Shoes		99.00
12/11	Hamiltons		87.00
12/11	K & W Shoes		93.50
12/11	Mary Lou's		150.00
12/12	The Shoe Stop		134.00
12/18	Joe Smith		15.00

	$2,332.50
Less Henrietta's refused C.O.D.	−78.00
	$2,254.50

Commissions: $225.45

Deductions:	Inv. #261 Samples	4.50
	Inv. #275 Personal	41.50
	Inv. #225 Personal	10.50
	Inv. #321 Personal	32.76
		$ 89.26

Enclosed:	$225.45
	−89.26
	$136.19

71. We send a commission statement to every sales rep once a month.

Consequently we hired about eight new people, started looking at houses because we didn't have room at our present place (we had leather in the kitchen, livingroom, and bedroom), and bought loads of leather.

To make a long story short, the guy turned out to be your basic crook. All but two or three small orders were phony. The stores didn't exist, or if they did they certainly didn't order any merchandise from him. At that time we didn't send out confirming orders, so we never knew this. We didn't ask the man for references, or even get a credit check on him. As it turned out he had a record as long as a giraffe's neck.

How did he take us? Not only did he get the commission money, he also get merchandise by telling us to ship some orders directly to him so he could have his men deliver them in person to get paid faster. He even sent us one or two small checks for the first couple of orders so we would think he was legit. He also sent in orders for stores with a P.O. box address. As it turned out, the name was phony — it was his box and he collected the merchandise. Where he fenced all the goods we still don't know. What we do know is we learned an expensive, but extremely valuable, lesson.

So be careful — get references, make credit checks, confirm all orders with the stores, and don't send commissions until orders are shipped. Any of these simple steps would have saved us about $3,000 in money and merchandise lost to this charming con artist.

HELPING YOUR SALES REP

You can help your sales rep sell by providing him with as much information as possible about your line. After all, he may know nothing about handcrafted silver jewelry, pottery, or leather. He needs to be able to answer questions buyers might ask. He needs to know why your product is good, what it's made out of, and how to care for it (see Figure 72).

You can also help him by servicing his accounts properly. Send out confirming orders immediately. If you promise two weeks delivery, make sure you ship within two weeks. Ship complete orders whenever possible. Keep the quality of goods shipped the same or better than the samples you provide to your reps.

Samples and Literature. We used to give free samples to sales reps, but this can get very costly. Now we charge them 40% off wholesale price. This way it at least takes care of our basic costs, and the rep can always find a place to sell them at that margin if he wants to. But we find that most reps don't get around to sending in the money and are just as happy if we deduct the cost of the samples from their commission checks. If they want extra merchandise for family, friends, and gifts, they get this strictly wholesale with their usual 10% commission. It wouldn't pay to give them this merchandise at 40% off, too.

Your reps will need a good sampling of your line, but remember they have other manufacturers' goods to carry so don't send them more than they can handle. Color photographs, ad sheets, catalogs, etc., will supplement the samples. Supply them with about 50 sets of all literature, price sheets, order forms, etc., to start with. From then on they'll let you know when they're running short. We also offer to have Holy Cow Leather business cards made for them if they want.

Keeping in Touch. Keep in touch with your sales reps as much as possible. Calling may be inconvenient because they're on the road a lot, so write often, telling them about new developments in your product line, asking how they're doing, what the reaction is to

Sales Information Sheet

Leather requires the proper handling and care to look its best. The more leather is worn, the more it improves its mellow look. Samples, however, which sit around and are not used, need to be taken care of properly. Don't leave them out where they can pick up dust. Don't crush or bend belts and bags. Keep bags filled with tissue or newspaper to give them a full look, as they will when filled by the customer who wears them. Don't throw belts into a suitcase or box but keep them rolled in neat circles. Occasionally a re-saddle soaping will bring life back to dull samples.

Our product sells best to the youth market. Call on junior departments, boutiques -- any place that caters to youth. Shoe stores, clothing stores, gift shops, department stores, and other specialty shops will also find a demand for it.

Our natural line of bags is made with yellow latigo. These bags are available with or without designs in two colors ONLY: Light Natural and Dark Natural. Natural bags cannot be ordered in any other colors. There are two small sizes: small round and small oblong; three medium sizes: round, square, and oblong; and one large size: saddle bag.

Our exquisite line of bags is made with russet latigo shoulder. This is more expensive leather, but can be dyed all the beautiful colors we offer. These bags are available in all colors, all designs, in small oblong, small round, square, round, and oblong sizes.

Our leather is hand-stamped, hand-dyed, and hand-laced. We use only top quality Fiebing leather dye -- no paints, acrylics, etc. It's guaranteed not to bleed, rub off, or crack. Exposure to direct sunlight for long periods of time will cause fading, which happens to any leather product. Saddle soap is recommended for care and cleaning.

A buyer may order a specific design and color or leave the assortment up to us. The flower design outsells all others.

72. This sales information sheet gives our reps the necessary information that will help them sell our line.

your product, how they think it might be improved, etc. Don't just sit and wonder why orders aren't coming in — get in touch and find out what's wrong. If a rep is having trouble selling your product, you want to know why. If it's simply the rep, then you'd better look for a replacement. But you'll find that since the reps are out in the field, they see what's selling, what the trends are, etc., and can give you some good advice.

By being in touch often, you also keep your product line on their minds. After all, they're representing several companies and yours is probably not the major source of income. So you have to keep trying to get their attention, convincing them that your line is worth pushing and profitable.

Terminating a Sales Rep. Usually it becomes obvious to both parties when a sales agreement should be terminated. If the rep isn't making sales, or is making only a few, sporadic sales, your line is hardly profitable to him. He may as well return the samples and drop your line. By the same token *you* don't want a rep who isn't selling. Neither of you are making any money from the relationship.

We've found that a simple letter stating these facts works out fine. If a rep has already paid for samples he may keep them or return them for credit. If he hasn't yet paid for them, of course you want these, plus literature, order forms, etc., returned. As soon as one agreement is terminated, a new rep can be started in that territory.

Incidentally, there are several reasons why a rep may not work out for you. Perhaps he sells to the kinds of stores that don't carry your merchandise. Perhaps your line doesn't fit in with the other lines he carries. Finally, he may just have found other lines that he can sell easier, and therefore has ignored yours. In any case, it's important to find out what's wrong and take action to correct it.

CHECKLIST

1. When you want to increase your wholesale sales and can offer a commission while still making a profit, consider getting one or more sales reps.

2. Advertise for reps or answer their ads in trade magazines and newspapers and look for them at trade shows.

3. Find out the going commission rate for your type of merchandise. Don't offer more or less.

4. Most reps want an exclusive territory of one or more states that they cover.

5. If you get a rep with a showroom, you *might* offer him a larger percentage or pay part of his showroom fees. If you do, make sure your line is well represented and pushed.

6. When a rep answers your ad, send him as much information about your product line as possible. Ask him for at least three references, preferably other manufacturers he represents, and have a credit check done on him.

7. The general procedure is to pay commissions monthly on all orders *shipped* the previous month.

8. When you receive an order from a rep, send out a confirming order to the store as soon as possible.

9. Provide reps with a set of samples. The usual charge is 40% or 50% off wholesale price. Provide literature, price lists, order forms, and business cards.

10. Give your reps as much information about your product as possible so they can answer buyers' questions and sell it better.

11. Keep in touch with your reps on a regular basis, especially if orders aren't coming in. Find out what's wrong immediately.

12. When a rep isn't selling your line, neither of you need the relationship. Terminate it and find someone else.

13. There *are* good reps. Keep looking until you find them. Then keep the lines of communication open and work together for bigger and better sales.

14

EXPANSION

There are probably some craftspeople who work strictly by themselves, and keep the level of their business the same year in and year out. They probably make a unique item and don't feel they can easily teach their craft to another person. If the demand for the product increases, customers simply have to wait longer for their order because only so many items can be produced within a given period of time.

But most of us aren't satisfied to keep selling the same amount we did the first six months. Our initial sales are small — we go to craft fairs every weekend, start to sell to a few shops on consignment, and then begin to sell wholesale. Eventually our orders are going to increase to the point where we have to hire people to help us, find a bigger workspace, and order larger quantities of raw materials. This is expansion.

THE NEED TO BE PROPERLY CAPITALIZED.

Under-capitalization means you don't have enough cash to work with. Maybe for the three months of heavy pre-Christmas sales your accounts receivable jumps from $3,000 to $9,000. In other words, you're shipping out three times as many orders as your normal capacity. This means paying more salaries, buying larger quantities of materials, and maybe even renting more workspace. This money must be laid out in advance, and even getting credit from your suppliers will only allow you another 30 days. Meanwhile it takes time for you to make the orders, ship them, and 30 or more days later, to receive payment from your accounts. Unless you have extra working capital or cash for these initial extra outlays, you're not going to make it through this period.

When you were shipping $3,000 per month, you were taking in $3,000 per month and perhaps spending $2,400 on expenses if your profit margin was 20%. When your sales suddenly increase to $9,000, you're spending $7,200 per month to fill these orders, but still only receiving $3,000 a month from previous sales. If you already have extra cash in the bank from your initial investment in the business, you'll have the working capital to meet this expansion. If you don't, you're going to need a loan to tide you over until these $9,000 sales start paying off.

The Risk of Expansion. Which should you increase first, capacity or orders? Some people would say, "Get the big orders first, then order more leather and move to larger quarters." However, if we get a big order for immediate shipment, it can't be done without enough leather, trained employees, or space to work in. If you're not ready for it, you might lose the order.

This is where the risk-taking comes into play. If you always have to be sure and have that big order in your hand before you'll make an expansion, either you won't get it or you won't be able to fill it properly. It takes time to buy or rent a bigger place, to hire and train new employees, and to have raw materials delivered. The time to expand your facilities is *before* you reach your top capacity in orders.

You can see the trends. If your top capacity is $1,000 worth of shipped orders per week utilizing all your employees, space, and regular material shipments, you know you can't handle any more business until you make some changes. If you're already receiving $1,000 worth of orders from your regular buyers, sales reps, etc., you can't expect to handle the Christmas boom. Or for another example, don't hire five new sales reps and sit back waiting for their orders to come in before expanding your production capacity. You need to be ready for those orders when they come in.

This is what we mean by risk. If you see a sales trend indicating that business will probably increase beyond your present capacity, move to larger quarters, hire more employees, and increase supply orders. Now, make sure business *does* increase. If orders don't start rolling in, then you'd better do something about it — whether it means more trade shows, more and better sales reps, more advertising, or whatever.

Machinery and Equipment Purchases. Sometime during your business growth you may find that a piece of machinery or equipment will really increase your efficiency, profit, and production potential. For example, we discovered after being in business awhile that buying a clicker machine that cuts out leather pieces would increase our potential. As long as we were cutting by hand our costs were higher, our production capacity was limited, and we just couldn't compete price-wise with our major competitors.

You may find that a new kiln, a potter's wheel, a loom, welding equipment, an industrial sewing machine, etc., may be the answer to your production problems. With it you'll be able to fill much larger orders, cut down your costs per item, and maybe even make a better product. The problem is, this machinery or equipment is very expensive to buy. It may be productive for the next 20 years and pay off enormously in the long run, but how do you get up the ready cash for it today? Unless you have it stashed away, some kind of loan is in order. This is another example of the need to be properly capitalized.

Developing New Products. Another need for expansion money arises when you want to change the products you now make, or add new ones. Costs could include new types of materials, more employees, new machinery and tools, and cost of time and labor in designing the new products.

Why bother developing new products? One reason we're now experiencing is that products often fade in popularity. For our first two years in business, hand-stamped latigo handbags were really in. Now they're not quite as popular; denim, canvas, and soft leathers are taking their place. This doesn't mean we can't sell hand-stamped latigo to *anyone*, but to maintain and increase our business growth we see a need to develop new types of leather handbags and new products that we don't have the capacity at present to produce. This means time will be spent investigating new machines and materials, designing new items, purchasing equipment such as an industrial sewing machine, buying new types of leather — and it all takes money.

Perhaps your craft is selling very well, but you want to expand into new areas for the challenge of working with different materials and products, or even just for faster business growth. This way, you avoid putting all your eggs in one basket — the more variety you have, the more your line will appeal to other markets. Of course you don't want to spread yourself too thin, either. Take each expansion one step at a time investing the proper research, know-how, and capital to make it work.

Retail Store. If you operate a successful retail store, opening a branch is another way to expand. If the city you're in can't support both stores, consider opening one in a neighboring town. In any case, research it carefully and try to make sure there are enough potential customers to support the additional shop. Then figure your costs for lease, fixtures, stock, labor, etc.; determine approximately how long you think it will take to get it on its feet. This will give a rough idea of the loan you'll need and the time it will take to repay.

If your wholesale business is doing well and you think a retail store in your town or city would also be profitable, this may be a viable way to expand. Check it out carefully, however. You may find it wasteful and costly to split your time and energy between the two operations.

GETTING CAPITAL FOR EXPANSION

After your business has been making a profit for a year or two and you've been able to leave some or all of this profit in the business, you'll have it to use for expansion purposes. Personal savings or loans from relatives are another possible source of capital. But be careful about borrowing money from relatives when they expect to be repaid within a short period of time. As pointed out earlier, it can take a long time for expansion to pay off. If you need a few thousand dollars to take you through a rush season, in a few months your accounts receivable and actual revenues will begin to match and you'll be able to repay your lender.

But if you're purchasing a piece of expensive equipment, buying a new building, or developing a new product line, these things could take years to pay off. In this case you need a long-term loan. If you have a relative willing to take the risk and wait this long, fine, but consider paying them interest at least equivalent to what they'd earn if they had their money in a savings bank for the same period of time. If you don't have a willing relative or friend, a bank loan is your next step.

Bank Loans. Whether you need a short-term or a long-term loan, don't be afraid to talk to your bank about it. Preferably go to one that you've already been doing your business and personal transactions with. They know you and your financial reliability from your checking and savings accounts, automobile loans, etc.

Bring your business records with you, including current income statements and balance sheets. Be prepared to give a brief but convincing account of why you need the money, how it will help your business, and when you'll be able to repay it. The more knowledgeable you sound, the better. Of course it helps to have been in the community for a while, to have a record of financial stability, to indicate sound business sense, show a record of business growth, etc.

If the amount of your loan request is too large or for some other reason the bank feels it can't comply, ask about a Small Business Association loan. You may find, in fact, that the bank suggests this alternative to you first. The Small Business Administration was set up by Congress in 1953 to help keep the small business community alive and thriving. One of their roles is to provide direct loans or to guarantee bank loans to small businesses for construction, expansion, conversion, purchase of machinery, equipment facilities, supplies or materials, and for working capital. For more information on S.B.A. loans and their publications, write to the Small Business Administration, Washington, D.C. 20416.

Obtaining an S.B.A. Loan. Since we recently received an S.B.A. loan through our bank, we can illustrate the forms and procedures necessary to obtain such a loan. The first step is to see your bank. We had previously obtained a small bank loan and repaid it, but since our new loan request was much larger, our bank suggested we proceed with an S.B.A. loan application.

First, you should decide exactly how much money you need and what it will be used for, such as $5,000 working capital, $3,000 clicker machine, etc. See Figure 73 for an illustration of our list accounting for $10,000 of purchases. We asked for an additional $5,000 for working capital.

Items to be Purchased

Renovations to present quarters ☐ (fixtures, electrical wiring, worktables)	$ 400
Cutting dies	3,000
Embossing dies	1,000
Riveting machine	100
Industrial sewing machine	1,000
Band saw	150
Leather ☐ 100 rolls latigo cowhide	2,000
☐ 300 vegetable tanned splits	2,350
	$10,000

---

73. This list of "Items To Be Purchased" is required for an S.B.A. loan. Another $5,000 was requested for working capital.

Projected Operating Statement: 1/1/74 - 12/31/74

Revenues

Wholesale Sales	$150,000	
Retail Store Sales	3,500	
Gross Sales	$153,500	
Less Cash Discounts	−3,000	
Net Sales	$150,500	$150,500

Manufacturing Expenses

Salaries	$ 30,702	
Contract Work	1,204	
Major Purchases (Materials)	49,665	
Minor Purchases (Materials)	6,622	
Gross Margin	$ 88,193	−$88,193

Other Expenses

Sales Commissions	$ 12,000	
Rent	1,800	
Promotion	5,000	
Freight	3,600	
Utilities	1,505	
Office Supplies and Postage	1,505	
Machinery Depreciation	500	
Retail Store Rent	1,505	
Retail Store Expenses	1,806	
Misc. Expenses	2,257	
	$ 31,478	−$31,478

Net Profit — $30,829

74. This is the projected operating statement Holy Cow Leather used in its S.B.A. loan application.

75. The front of S.B.A. Form 413, Personal Financial Statement.

Section 3. Other Stocks and Bonds: Give listed and unlisted Stocks and Bonds *(Use separate sheet if necessary)*

No. of Shares	Names of Securities	Cost	Market Value Statement Date	
			Quotation	Amount

Section 4. Real Estate Owned. *(List each parcel separately. Use supplemental sheets if necessary. Each sheet must be identified as a supplement to this statement and signed). (Also advises whether property is covered by title insurance, abstract of title, or both).*

Title is in name of	Type of property

Address of property (City and State)	Original Cost to (me) (us) $_____
	Date Purchased _____
	Present Market Value $_____
	Tax Assessment Value $_____

Name and Address of Holder of Mortgage (City and State)	Date of Mortgage _____
	Original Amount $_____
	Balance $_____
	Maturity _____
	Terms of Payment _____

Status of Mortgage, i.e., current or delinquent. If delinquent describe delinquencies

Section 5. Other Personal Property. *(Describe and if any is mortgaged, state name and address of mortgage holder and amount of mortgage, terms of payment and if delinquent, describe delinquency.)*

Section 6. Other Assets. *(Describe)*

Section 7. Unpaid Taxes. *(Describe in detail, as to type, to whom payable, when due, amount, and what, if any, property a tax lien, if any, attaches)*

Section 8. Other Liabilities. *(Describe in detail)*

(I) or (We) certify the above and the statements contained in the schedules herein is a true and accurate statement of (my) or (our) financial condition as of the date stated herein. This statement is given for the purpose of: *(Check one of the following)*

☐ Inducing S.B.A. to grant a loan as requested in application, of the individual or firm whose name appears herein, in connection with which this statement is submitted.

☐ Furnishing a statement of (my) or (our) financial condition, pursuant to the terms of the guaranty executed by (me) or (us) at the time S.B.A. granted a loan to the individual or firm, whose name appears herein.

_____ Signature   _____ Signature   _____ Date

SBA FORM 413 (8-67)   Page 2   GPO 1967 O—274-284

76. The back of S.B.A. Form 413, Personal Financial Statement.

You'll have to provide copies of balance sheets and income (operating) statements for every year of the business and a current balance sheet (within the last three months). If your business is new, or if past operating statements don't indicate enough profit to cover the loan, prepare a projected operating statement for the following year indicating what you expect sales, costs, and profit to be (see Figure 74).

You'll also be asked to fill out a "personal financial statement," that should include the assets and liabilities of your spouse, if any. In fact you'll find that banks and the S.B.A. will usually require that husband and wife apply for the loan jointly, even if only one is the proprietor of the business (see Figures 75 and 76).

For each and every manager of the business, a description of their education, technical training, employment and business experience will have to be written up (see Figure 77).

You'll also be required to write up a history and description of the business, explaining when and how the business was started, what its purpose is, its growth and development, etc. (see Figure 78). Finally, you'll have to write up the benefits your company will receive from the loan (see Figure 79).

Other items you may be required to furnish are insurance on the manager or managers of the business until the loan is repaid and a chattel mortgage on equipment or property used to secure the loan. Your banker will explain the various aspects of the loan requirements and tell you which ones you're responsible for. Ask him questions about any items you're uncertain about.

Repaying a Loan. A small loan of $500.00 to $3,000 for a short-term investment of materials and labor for a seasonal sales growth can probably be paid back within three to six months. There are short-term business loans where the interest is a set rate per year. You pay interest on the exact time you have the money, and the whole amount is due on the end-date with interest.

For larger loans, especially S.B.A. loans, the repayment periods are longer and usually made in monthly payments. We took our loan for three years, but our banker told us the most common loan period is five years. The length you'll take depends on the amount of money, the purpose you're using it for, and the company's financial ability to repay. Give yourself enough time. You can always pay back the loan sooner and save the extra interest, but it often takes longer than you think for expansion investments to pay off.

Summing Up. Think about an expansion loan *before* you find yourself in a situation where you can't pay your suppliers on time because of lack of working capital. Don't jeopardize your good credit rating or take the chance of going bankrupt simply because you're afraid to ask your bank for a loan. When sales seem to be increasing and your purchasing needs become larger, plan your money needs ahead of time.

Don't be afraid to ask a bank for too small a loan either. If you only need $500.00 or $1,000 for a month or two, talk to your banker. By paying back this small loan on time, you demonstrate financial stability and wise planning. As your needs grow, your bank will help you meet them based on your past performance.

Many small businesses have been started or helped along the way by a loan. Don't let a fear of borrowing money stop your business from growing and thriving.

Lyn Taetzsch
President, Holy Cow Leather

Lyn Taetzsch has a B.A. in English from Rutgers University.
She has a strong background in art, having attended Cooper
Union Art School for two years, having had a one-person art
show in NYC, plus numerous other showings. Her art background has equipped her to design all the leather articles
made by Holy Cow Leather, mix her own dye colors, etc. In
addition she spent three months at her sister's leather shop
in California learning all she could about the leather
business before starting her own in May of 1972.

Lyn worked for 3 years as office manager in a firm of sales
representatives in New Jersey. She composed her own sales
letters, quotations, etc., and learned a lot here about the
operation of a sales office. She worked for $2\frac{1}{2}$ years as
office manager of an importing firm where she took care of
inventory control books, general bookkeeping, invoices, etc.

Her most recent experience before starting her own business
was managing a training program for disadvantaged workers at
Blue Cross/Blue Shield in Newark, New Jersey. Here she
trained employees in office methods, supervised staff,
developed training programs, and wrote government contracts.

*77. You'll have to write up a description of background and experience, such as this one,
of each manager in the business.*

Holy Cow Leather History and Description

Holy Cow Leather was registered as a proprietorship by Lyn
Taetzsch on May 16, 1972. The purpose of the business was to
make handcrafted leather belts, handbags, and small accessories and to sell them wholesale. For the first year Lyn
worked at the business by herself, making her own items and
selling them to retail shops within a 100-mile radius of
Ithaca, New York.

In the spring of 1973 Lyn hired several sales representatives in other parts of the country to represent her line of
leather on a commission basis. At that time she also showed
the line at the International Leather Goods Show in NYC.
These developments increased sales and it became necessary
to hire employees and to move to larger quarters.

In June of 1973 Lyn and her husband Herb Genfan bought a
ranch home in Newfield, New York. Utilizing the basement
and a finished garage room, they set up the business here
and hired several employees. A clicker machine was purchased
that summer to facilitate cutting of the leather, thereby
allowing a much increased production.

Gradually more employees were hired, more sales representatives contracted, until at this point Holy Cow Leather has
10 employees and 11 sales representatives throughout the
country. Sales increased from approximately $6,000 the
first year of operations to $66,000 the second year of
operations.

*78. Another item required is a history and description of the business itself, such as this
one about Holy Cow Leather.*

Loan Benefits

One of the problems the business has had is keeping enough working capital in order to make timely payments to suppliers, order sufficient advance quantities of leather, pay advance fees for trade shows, purchase advertising materials, etc. The loan would enable the business to have this working capital.

Lyn is also planning to expand the line of goods offered in order to be more competitive, attract better sales representatives, and generally increase sales. In order to do this, money is needed to purchase machinery and equipment, new kinds of leather, cutting and embossing dies, etc. The loan will enable her to do this, thereby greatly increasing the business' profit potential.

79. This is a write-up of the benefits Holy Cow Leather would receive from the S.B.A. loan. You'll be required to write up a similar explanation for your application.

CHECKLIST

1. To increase sales, you must increase your expenditures for labor, materials, and workspace. This expansion takes money, or capital. If you don't have it, you'll be forced to refuse additional orders, stay small, or go bankrupt because of inability to pay suppliers.

2. Don't wait too long to increase your capacity. When you see the trend moving toward more and larger sales, get ready for it in advance. Hire and train new employees, order more supplies and obtain more workspace.

3. If orders don't start flowing in as expected after expansion, go out and get them. Go to trade shows, hire more sales reps, replace bad reps with good reps, get advertising, etc.

4. At some point you may find a particular machine or piece of equipment will allow you to expand production, efficiency, and profits. To purchase it, you'll probably need a loan.

5. Developing new products is another reason for getting a loan. Increasing the variety of items you produce will put you in a more competitive, secure position.

6. If you operate a successful retail store, opening up a branch in a neighboring town or shopping plaza may provide opportunity for growth. But you'll need the capital to do it.

7. Personal savings, capital from business profits, and loans from relatives, if available, are usually the cheapest way to obtain capital.

8. If none of the above is available, try the bank you normally do business with. Go prepared with income statements, balance sheets, and sound reasons for wanting the loan.

9. If you're unable to get a loan directly through your bank, apply for a Small Business Administration loan. Your banker will help you fill out their forms and meet their requirements.

10. Give yourself enough time to repay a loan. You can always pay it back early and thereby save the interest you would have paid.

15

EMPLOYEES

When we started our own craft business, still working in the garage and lacing a few bags while watching television, we used to joke about building a factory, hiring employees, and having a comptroller, personnel director, a few vice-presidents, and an executive vice-president to oversee all the vice-presidents. Of course we still joke about it, but who knows?

DO YOU NEED EMPLOYEES?

You'll find out a curious thing about the manufacturing end of a business — unless it grows, it doesn't just stay small, it loses out to the ones that *are* growing. There are improvements you can make that only size will allow, such as buying supplies in large quantities, setting up efficient production lines and systems, and even enhancing your reputation and ability to serve more and larger customers. There's nothing quite as frustrating as saying "No" to a big chain of stores when they say, "Can you make 500 of those a month?" Once the business bug gets you, you'll find yourself trying to say "Yes" to the next buyer who makes that kind of offer.

But you can't do it alone. If you're growing in small steps, sooner or later you'll need help. At first, one of your neighbors may do fine. He or she likes your work, is pretty handy and artistic, and could use the extra few dollars you'll pay for help. Neighbors and friends are sufficient in the beginning, but in time you'll run out of them and need a few other willing hands.

Finding Employees. Crafts are a special kind of business. Usually you'll look for a certain esthetic sense, a good head, and in production, the motivation to endure repeated operations. We've found that a college town probably supplies the largest pool of available talent in one place. Salary, particularly at first, isn't going to be very large, so a college student also fits the bill here. Either he's in school and needs a part-time job, or is still hanging around the town until he's able to go on to more formal training or a career. Some, of course, may stay with you for years, growing in responsibility, know-how, and income as you do.

Even if you're not in a college town, you shouldn't have much trouble finding someone to work with you. Although we haven't had to try other employment pools, there are many other sources, such as the aged, handicapped, high-school students, youth clubs, and friends. There's no reason why, with a good selection process, you shouldn't find some very good employees in any town. There are probably a lot of people who would prefer your basement, garage, or small shop over the typical blue-collar, secretarial, or even white-collar job. There's an indescribable *esprit* in a craft shop that will help you attract employees.

Recruiting. The techniques of recruiting employees are few and simple. To get a few neighbors to work with you, you can chat with them personally. For college or high-school students, you can go to school placement offices. Most schools have counselors or well-staffed career offices that will be happy to post your help-wanted notices on bulletin boards. The service is free and the results very good. As with any notice of employment, you're under no obligation to hire if, after an interview, you don't wish to. And unless you're an impossible boss, you can use school services over and over again.

Another way is by word of mouth — and it's still free. Once you have an employee or two, you'll be asked if you have more work for one of their friends. Referrals from employees have a distinct advantage. It implies your employees like the work and the shop enough to have their friends work there also, and if your employee likes it and does it well, his interested friends will often be as happy and as good a worker as he is. Word of mouth referrals are usually a sign of a good shop.

Paid advertisements are also effective. Newspapers in smaller towns charge as little as $3.00 an ad in the help-wanted column, depending upon the size of the ad and circulation of the paper. Here you've got to be able to state your needs in a few words. In crafts, if you need someone experienced, you can specify something like, "Pottery people to work wheel, kiln experience required," or "Leatherworkers to stamp and dye handcrafted belts, bags, etc." If you want to train an inexperienced employee, you can reach a larger group by adding a phrase like, "Will train." Your reason for being specific is to avoid wasting time in explaining the job to many who are unqualified and would answer a more vague ad like "Workers wanted in craft shop." The clearest ad allows the job seeker to choose or reject ads that don't fit. With any ad you'll find some who think they can do your job but really can't, so the more precise you are, the better.

The Job Description. A clear ad presupposes a clear idea in your mind of what you'd like an employee to do. When your business has grown past the one-of-a-kind project stage and is now in a stage of mass production, you may have to break down the total product into simplified steps. You know the whole process, but not everyone you hire will. And you may prefer, as most businesses do, to have a person perform only one step, developing speed and expertise by repetition. In leather, for example, you'll find Jim is a great cutter, but can't really tell oxblood dye from red. Since Jim likes cutting, he does it, and someone else handles the leather dyes. The important thing in producing quantity is to break down the total job into easily learned steps. In making a belt, for example, the hide must be cut into strips, holes punched, sides edged, design stamped, dyed, buckled and riveted, finished and coated, and finally placed into stock or packed for an order. Each of these steps can be easily taught, but only if you've taken the time to list the steps.

Such a list, literally a job description, is an invaluable aid not only in placing ads for help, but in training new employees, in timing parts of the job for piece rates (to be discussed later), and in knowing how to figure your costs and how many employees to hire for a certain amount of production. The successful businessperson has a job description or list of duties for every job from sweeper to senior vice-president. The job description also allows employees to know just what they're expected to do. So the time spent in preparing such lists of tasks is continually paid off during the life of your business. Also, with a clear knowledge of what you want an employee to do, your ad will be succinct — brief and effective.

SELECTING EMPLOYEES

Even the best ad won't do the whole job. You still have to see the applicants and interview them, formally or informally. The interview can be a pleasant exchange of information. Prospective employees want to find out about the hours, the pay, the actual workplace, the duties, and how you seem to come across as a possible boss. You, naturally, want to know their availability (full or part-time), get some idea of their reliability by how they come across to you, and of course, find out what skills they have. An interview will give you and the applicant a fair idea of what you're both getting into.

To check out potential skill or dexterity, we've added a practical test to the interview. Crafts require some decent eye-hand coordination and we think we can discover this by having the applicant make a small article, such as a key ring, right at the interview. It takes only a few minutes to discover how a person holds a tool, if he can place a design in the center of an object, if he follows directions, and even to a degree, his sense of creativity. It will also give the applicant an opportunity to see if he or she will want to do the work. If it's at all possible, we believe it's useful to give such a test before deciding on the applicant. We find we've insulted no one and have proven to "non-hires" that they can't do what we require. Those who "passed" and are working for us recall it as "kind of cute" or at worst "funny."

Job Application. Besides our little key ring test, we ask each applicant to fill out a job application form (see Figure 80). We use the information on the form to start off our interview. Previous work experience, no matter what kind, can be very useful. The fact that an applicant has held a job in the past means he or she has taken on a responsibility and is familiar with the discipline and regularity of working.

We also ask about previous art and craft experience. Usually a person who likes, or who has experience in, this area will also enjoy and be good at working with leather. The name, address, and phone number are for a permanent record and so you can get in touch with the person when a decision has been made. Since we have full-time and part-time people working, we need to know the hours the applicant can work so we can figure out how to schedule him in. During the interview we also jot down on the application any other information we think is important.

The Interview. We feel that motivation is as important as skill. During the interview chat you should try to delve into this. Motivation simply means, "Why do you want to do this kind of work?" If you believe it's just to get a few bucks together to pay this month's rent you may still want to hire the person. But it isn't likely that you'll get a satisfied, long-term employee. Clearly you hope to hear a plausible response that allows you to predict some success and reliability — "I've done a little leather" or "I used to throw a

Holy Cow Leather Job Application

Name: _____

Address: _____

Telephone: _____

Previous Work Experience:

Name of Company _____

Period worked: From _____ To _____

Type of work: _____

Name of Company _____

Period worked: From _____ To _____

Type of work: _____

Name of Company _____

Period worked: From _____ To _____

Type of work: _____

Have you taken any related courses, such as in art, crafts,

etc.? Describe if you have: _____

Have you done any leatherwork, crafts, sewing, woodworking,

etc. before? If so, describe: _____

What hours do you want to work each week? _____

80. We use this job application form at Holy Cow Leather, but you can devise one to fit your particular needs.

few pots just for friends, and I need some money to help pay my tuition." Whatever the reason, we want to feel reassured by the applicant that he wants to do this kind of work for a reasonable period of time and will be satisfied while doing it.

The process of selecting the right person isn't a science no matter how many tests you give nor how skilled an interviewer you are. You'll want to use the method that works best, but don't fret over mistakes. Some people won't work out, and some will be great at first but then give up. Others will be slow starters but turn out to be the most organized and skillful in the shop. We warn you of only two things. Don't form prejudices without observation. For instance, you may not *think* women can lift a roll of leather or throw clay for two hours at a stretch, but they can, and do, quite well. And the reverse — you may not believe a thick-fingered guy can drop a speck of dye into just the right flower design, but he can and does.

The second thing we advise is not to look for perfection in those you hire. Your decision isn't irrevocable, and you can, with sensitivity, fire as well as hire. A person may even quit of his own accord if it doesn't work out.

Once you've worked with a few employees, a bit of observation will help you select the next ones. What kinds of personalities get along? Just how much strength is needed for throwing clay? Can a person do one job all day, or should we hire someone who can fill in?

TRAINING

The best workers are not only self-motivated, but well-trained and supervised. A new employee who has already worked in the same craft must still be trained. By definition, craft is personal. You do things just a bit differently than the next person. You use the tool a certain way because you've found it takes less time, saves the tool, and is less fatiguing. Even if the new employee does it exactly the same way, he still knows nothing about your systems, your division of work, and your inventory needs. He must learn about your clean-up requirements, policies or rules, and your particular way of doing things.

We hope we've stressed enough the need for training; because without it you can expect everything to go wrong that possibly could. Foul-ups are so prevalent in industry that this concept has been given a name. "Murphy's Law" states that "Anything that can go wrong, will." We've never been able to discover who Murphy was, but nonetheless we admire his perspicacity. Training and supervision will help reduce the effect of his observation.

Training Methods. Part of the training of a new person is to show him where things are, give him the over-all picture, advise him of some initial "rules," and introduce him around. Commonly called orientation and induction, the time is well spent and will make him feel at ease. Also included under training is on-the-job instruction in each task he's to do. You may instruct him yourself or you may prefer someone else for the job, but be sure instruction is done well. Typically, a manual job is performed by the instructor with the trainee watching closely. Then the trainee repeats to the instructor what he's going to do. If he misses a point, the instructor corrects him and lets him go on. Then the trainee actually performs the operation, is corrected if need be, and continues on. This three-part method can be repeated, tactfully, and comfortably, allowing for some nervousness at first. When you feel your newcomer has it down, no matter how slow at first, you can get out of his way for a while and let him continue practicing.

Then follow-up by watching him and refining your instructions. Let him know what speed and quality you require. If he feels confident and you see he's doing it correctly, go away again. This time come back in half an hour or so and answer his questions, show him some additional points, and perhaps correct his technique if he's forgotten. This, with whatever variations fit your craft, is training for routine operations. It won't produce a skilled artisan, but it will produce a skilled operator. Only time, talent, and a close relationship will develop a fine craftsperson. But apprentice or craftsperson, the person you hire will need the kind of training just described for each job you want him to do. Here again, the time spent in careful instruction will pay you and your employee back a hundredfold in safe, quality production.

SUPERVISING

Yesterday you were a self-employed, sole-proprietor craftsperson, working all by yourself. Today you supervise others — you're a "boss." Orders are increasing and you can predict a good return for your efforts. You need help to grow and you really want to grow. So you have employees, people who are happy to see you make it and to grow with you. But they can't do it without you. Unless you have a business composed of completely equal working partners (and some companies are organized just that way, successfully), you probably have a wider awareness of how many orders are in, predicted sales, the markets for your product, the supplies, raw materials, prices, and so on. Also, as the owner you're the one risking your capital, and as creator of the company you give a personal direction to the business. You probably have more knowledge and facts with which to make decisions than any other member of your group. Or you may hire someone as a manager, provide him or her with the information and delegate supervision. In any event, supervision is a must.

Supervision can be defined as organizing, planning, directing, coordinating, communicating, innovating, budgeting, controlling, and a host of similar words. Writers and practitioners in the field of management consistently use these words in their descriptions, and they're all important and meaningful. A good supervisor must plan the production, organize the work and the employees to keep a good flow of production, direct others, and give instructions. He must budget time, money, supplies, and people effectively. It's also important to be a good communicator. What we've found is that we *know* all the things a supervisor should be, but it's easier said than done. There are countless books on the functions of management, but precious few that reveal the attitude or the psychological frame of mind that you need to perform these functions.

What we've discovered and rediscovered each time we've failed, is that most of us are either too soft or too hard. Neither attitude works, and oddly enough, more of us suffer from the "too soft" approach. A lot of "bosses" may seem like the whip-cracking type, but then again, a lot of bosses are pretty poor managers. More often you'll meet (or be) the kind of person who just can't say "No" or "I'll have to let you go." We've discovered that every time we try to avoid what we think will hurt someone, we end up hurting both him and ourselves.

The Proper Attitude. Let's see if we can nail down what we call "attitude" a bit more specifically. We've said your employees need you and your supervision. Without your knowledge and direction they can't begin to work. Without your standards of quality, of safety, of quantity, etc., they can't produce. And, without their abilities and their suggestions, you can't produce. But none of these things happen without communication. That is, if you don't tell them what you want, when you want it, and how you want it, it won't be done.

So you, as a supervisor, owe it to your employees and to your business to tell people what you want and need. Of all the reasons for failure, fear of expressing one's desires lies at the root of unsuccessful managerial performance most of the time. We often don't believe we have the right to ask for what we would like. But it's imperative to demand what we know is appropriate, and not to tolerate the behavior of those who won't or can't comply after training.

Using the Proper Attitude. As harsh as this may sound we still aren't advocating that you be the cigar-chomping, bellowing, slave-driver type of boss. For example, in the context of safety, we have every right to prohibit an employee from smoking while pouring gasoline or lighting a gas kiln. And we therefore have every right, after instruction and admonition, to ask the person to change his behavior in that one specific act, or, if he can't or won't, to leave.

Let's say you have an employee that tries hard and needs the job but manages to ruin as much good leather as he or she saves. And after careful instruction the person still wastes material. Are you able to warn him that he'll be fired if there's no improvement and fire him after, say, three such warnings? If you can, then you're becoming a good supervisor.

Or let's say that every other week he calls in sick, or says his cat died, or says he has to go to Indianapolis to see his sister. In your planning, you count on him to help produce a certain number of orders. You could run around and try to get a temporary replacement every time he disappoints you, but you'll save more time by chatting with him about your need for greater reliability. If, after you've set a date for improvement and he still continues such behavior, simply fire him and replace him with someone who is healthy, has a healthy cat, and whose sister lives nearby.

In order to keep a business alive you can't expect employees to read your mind. You owe people direct and clear expressions of what you require or they have a perfect right to do exactly as they were doing. It can be done tactfully, without anger, and with a sensitive respect for the other person's value system — but it must be done.

Positive Communication. We've been putting a lot of stress on telling employees that you want them to change, or improve. However, there's just as much need for positive reinforcement. When the group has really worked hard and gotten out a lot of rush orders, tell them what a great job they've done. If a new employee begins to improve his skill and production capacity, let him know what progress he's making. When your employees know you'll honestly express both positive and negative feelings about their work, they'll respect your opinion and work harder to meet your requests.

When you respect your own right to express your needs, and respect the other person's ability to respond in an adult manner to your expression, you're communicating. There's always a risk that he may take offense, but if you're aware of what you want to communicate, you'll almost always get a positive response. Our own research shows that most of the time the person finds our requests quite acceptable, changes his behavior in the direction we requested, and even feels better and more secure in his ability to do things well. In addition, we feel less hostile because we've told them, they *do* know, and we both have a healthier relationship.

Nevertheless, we still fail time and time again, but we keep trying. We'll probably never become completely proficient in owning our own feelings and in communicating precisely what we're experiencing, but we can work toward it, encourage it in those with whom we're involved, and end up with a better, more productive relationship. (For some additional points on this subject note two authors in the bibliography, Carl Rogers and David W. Johnson.)

Salary — Piecework or Time. In Chapter 2, Pricing, you'll note that a certain percentage of the price of each product is allocated for labor. For example, if a belt wholesales for $5.00, 67¢ may be allocated for labor. Here's how we arrive at this figure: it takes 20 minutes to make the belt, employees are paid $2.00 per hour, 20 minutes is 1/3 of an hour, so 1/3 of $2.00 is 67¢. Now to make certain that the labor for every belt costs us exactly 67¢ we could pay employees by piecework. For every belt they made they would be paid 67¢. Those who made exactly three belts an hour would earn $2.00 per hour. Those who worked faster would make more.

We did start out by paying on a piecework basis, but it's more complex than it seems. No one makes a complete belt from start to finish. One person may put all the designs on 50 belts, another may dye 50 belts, and another may put the buckles on. So we had to break down the 20 minutes into each step: stamping design, 5 minutes; buckling, 2½ minutes, etc. We then made up a list of each separate job and its corresponding pay rate so employees would know how fast they had to do a particular job in order to earn $2.00 per hour. The original 20 minutes for the whole belt was based on how fast we ourselves could make one at a normal pace. So we assumed the new employee would probably earn less than $2.00 per hour until he became more experienced and could work more quickly.

Piecework was satisfactory for awhile, but one of the problems was that in trying to obtain speed, quality was often overlooked. Also, poor workers earned so little it was a waste of time for them and they wasted our workspace by being there. Piecework didn't allow for odd things that came up, such as a tool breaking, cleaning up, differences in leather, mixing more dye, etc.

We've since switched to time-rates. We start new employees at $1.80 per hour for their first 80 hours, assuming this is a "breaking in" period. Then they move up to $2.00 per hour if they prove satisfactory during that first 80 hours. Everyone has their good and bad days, some are better at certain tasks, some learn more quickly, and some have more stamina, but in general we find that an employee worth keeping is worth paying the $2.00 per hour. He'll get faster with experience, good training, and good supervision.

The hourly rate you pay will depend on several factors — minimum wage laws, the "going rate" in your community, abundance of potential employees, and what you can afford. Our employees know we're a young company, that we're not making huge profits, and that we try to be fair about our pay standards. While none of them are living high off what we pay them, they're able to earn the money they need at a job they enjoy, or they wouldn't be here.

CONCLUSION

A discussion of employees can't be separated from a discussion of supervisors: either the two work intelligently together as self-motivated beings who agree to cooperate for certain values neither can obtain alone, or they produce nothing and must part company. Employee's ideas, if you show you want them, can help a business grow just as surely as a supervisor's ideas. Employees make the product. Your job as a supervisor is to create an environment in which they can not only produce the goods, but in which they can find satisfaction in what they do.

CHECKLIST

1. When you find that your work alone can't produce enough to fill all your orders, you need employees.

2. You can find employees through friends and neighbors, school placement offices, organizations for handicapped, aged, youth, employee referrals, and paid advertisements.

3. Use a job description (a list of exactly what the employee will be expected to do) as basis for writing up the ad and telling the applicant what the job is all about.

4. At the interview, use an application form, a practical test (if possible), and personal discussion to ascertain the applicant's potential and interest in the job.

5. Train every new employee thoroughly in each task. This includes a general orientation his first day and continuous follow-through thereafter.

6. Supervise your employees with continuous communication — be aware of what's happening, express your needs and gripes, praise sincerely when work is done well, and utilize feedback from employees.

7. Pay rates, whether piece or time, will depend on minimum wage laws, "going rates" in your area, abundance of potential employees, and what you can afford.

8. A good, communicative employee-employer relationship is vital to your business. Don't neglect it.

16

PAYROLL TAXES, FORMS, AND INSURANCE

No matter how many strangers or friends you hire, whether full-time or part-time, you'll be responsible for taxes, forms, and insurance requirements. First, all the federal forms and taxes will apply to you. Next, depending upon the city and state you're in, you'll be responsible for state, and possibly city, taxes and forms. Contact your local agencies and get information about your responsibilities *before* you hire any employees. Ask them to send you the necessary forms, timetables for filing, etc., so you'll be prepared. If you don't understand exactly what your responsibilities are after reading their booklets, call the agency and ask them. There are penalties and fees for late filing of these taxes and forms, and it's illegal not to pay them at all.

REGISTERING WITH TAX AGENCIES

If you plan to hire employees, get in touch with all your local tax agencies and notify them. The Internal Revenue Service will send you a form that must be filled out to receive an Employer's Identification Number. You'll use this number on all future federal, state and city tax forms. The I.R.S. will also send you an Employer's Tax Guide that will give you all the information you need to know about how and when to deduct and pay federal withholding taxes, social security taxes (F.I.C.A. or F.O.A.B.), and federal unemployment taxes. They'll also send you the necessary forms for deposits, reporting, etc.

Next call your state agencies and tell them you'll soon be a new employer. Ask them to send you all the necessary forms, and information about withholding and unemployment taxes. If your city has withholding taxes, call them also. You can find all these agencies in your phone book. Look under United States Government for the Internal Revenue Service, your state government for state tax agencies, and your city government for city tax agencies.

WORKMEN'S COMPENSATION AND DISABILITY INSURANCE

If you have one or more employees working on your premises, you're probably required by state law to have Workmen's Compensation and Disability Insurance. Check with your state Workmen's Compensation Board or your insurance company to find out how these laws work in your state.

Basically, workmen's compensation pays for employee medical bills incurred from an accident at work. For example, one of our employees cut himself badly with a knife while cutting out leather belts. He was driven to the emergency room of the hospital, where he received several stitches. We filled out the necessary forms and workmen's compensation paid for the hospital costs. It also paid him a percentage of the salary he lost since he was unable to return to work for several days after the accident.

Workmen's disability insures employees of at least part of their salary if they're unable to return to work due to some disability incurred on the job. Both these insurance policies protect the worker. Check the laws in your state.

FORMS FOR EMPLOYEES

On the first day of work each employee must fill out a Form W-4 or W-4E, Employee's Withholding Allowance Certificate (see Figures 81 and 82). You as the employer should keep these forms in your files. You'll use this information in computing the employee's taxes when making out his paycheck. Most employees will use a W-4 Form, but those who for some reason feel they'll incur no liability for federal income tax that year may fill out W-4E. In this case you won't deduct any federal income taxes from their pay.

Figure 83 illustrates the front and back of Form IT-2104, New York State Employee's Withholding Exemption Certificate. If your business is located in a city or state that withholds payroll taxes, your employees will be required to fill out a certificate similar to this also. Keep enough of these forms on hand at all times so you'll be ready whenever you hire a new employee.

PAYROLL BOOK

At your local office-supply store, pick up a payroll book. They come in various sizes, depending on the number of employees you have (see Figure 84). Note that it's set up for a weekly payroll period, The hours each employee worked are listed for each day. There's a column to enter total time, regular rate of pay, and extra for overtime, etc. We have our employees write down their hours on a separate piece of paper each day. At the end of the pay period, we collect the time sheets and transfer the hours to the payroll book.

Once we've multiplied the hourly rate by the total hours, we're ready to figure out the deductions. F.O.A.B. (also known as F.I.C.A., or social security) is computed by multiplying a set percentage rate times the earnings. This percentage rate, presently 5.85% for employees, may change over the years. A table is provided in the Employer's Tax Guide that saves you the trouble of computing it. The same guide is used no matter what the exemptions or marital status of an employee.

Federal withholding tax can be figured out from the tax tables provided in the Employer's Tax Guide, but here you have to watch for marital status and number of

Employee's Withholding Allowance Certificate

The explanatory material below will help you determine your correct number of withholding allowances, and will indicate whether you should complete the new Form W–4 at the bottom of this page.

How Many Withholding Allowances May You Claim?

Please use the schedule below to determine the number of allowances you may claim for tax withholding purposes. In determining the number, keep in mind these points: If you are single and hold more than one job, you may not claim the same allowances with more than one employer at the same time; If you are married and both you and your wife or husband are employed, you may not claim the same allowances with your employers at the same time. A nonresident alien other than a resident of Canada, Mexico or Puerto Rico may claim only one personal allowance.

Figure Your Total Withholding Allowances Below

(a) Allowance for yourself—enter 1 . . . . _1_

(b) Allowance for your wife (husband)—enter 1 . . . . _—_

(c) Allowance for your age—if 65 or over—enter 1 . . . . _—_

(d) Allowance for your wife's (husband's) age—if 65 or over—enter 1 . . . . _—_

(e) Allowance for blindness (yourself)—enter 1 . . . . _—_

(f) Allowance for blindness (wife or husband)—enter 1 . . . . _—_

(g) Allowance(s) for dependent(s)—you are entitled to claim an allowance for each dependent you will be able to claim on your Federal income tax return. Do not include yourself or your wife (husband)* . . . . . _—_

(h) Special withholding allowance—if you have only one job, and do not have a wife or husband who works— enter 1 . . . . _—_

(i) Total—add lines (a) through (h) above . . . . _1_

If you do not plan to itemize deductions on your income tax return, enter the number shown on line (i) on line 1, Form W–4 below. Skip lines (j) and (k).

(j) Allowance(s) for itemized deductions—If you do plan to itemize deductions on your income tax return, enter the number from line 5 of worksheet on back . . . . _—_

(k) Total—add lines (i) and (j) above. Enter here and on line 1, Form W–4 below . . . . _1_

*If you are in doubt as to whom you may claim as a dependent, see the instructions which came with your last Federal income tax return or call your local Internal Revenue Service office.

See Table and Worksheet on Back if You Plan to Itemize Your Deductions

Completing New Form W–4

If you find that you are entitled to one or more allowances in addition to those which you are now claiming, please increase your number of allowances by completing the form below and filing with your employer. If the number of allowances you previously claimed decreases, you must file a new Form W–4 within 10 days. (Should you expect to owe more tax than will be withheld, you may use the same form to increase your withholding by claiming fewer or "0" allowances on line 1 or by asking for additional withholding on line 2 or both.)

▼ Give the bottom part of this form to your employer; keep the upper part for your records and information ▼

Form **W-4** (Rev. Aug. 1972) Department of the Treasury Internal Revenue Service	**Employee's Withholding Allowance Certificate** (This certificate is for income tax withholding purposes only; it will remain in effect until you change it.)

Type or print your full name MARY SUE SMITH	Your social security number 120 - 40 - 3482
Home address (Number and street or rural route) 105 MAIN ST.	**Marital status** ☒ Single ☐ Married
City or town, State and ZIP code OURTOWN, NEBRASKA 10253	(If married but legally separated, or wife (husband) is a nonresident alien, check the single block.)

1 Total number of allowances you are claiming . . . . | _1_

2 Additional amount, if any, you want deducted from each pay (if your employer agrees) . . . . | $ —

I certify that to the best of my knowledge and belief, the number of withholding allowances claimed on this certificate does not exceed the number to which I am entitled.

Signature ▶ *Mary Sue Smith*   Date ▶ 2/1/74   19____

---

81. Every employee should fill out a W-4 or W-4E Form on the first day of work.

82. A Form W-4E is for those employees who don't expect to incur any liability for federal withholding taxes during the year.

83. Form IT-2104 must be filled out by New York State employees on or before their first day on the job.

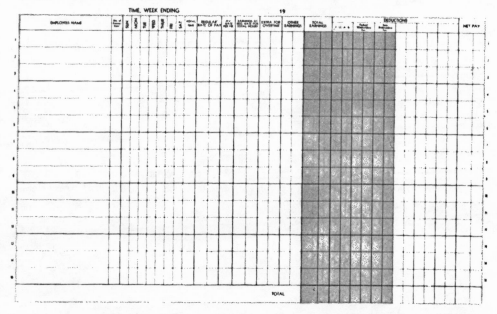

84. *On this blank page from a payroll book, notice that there are spaces to record employee hours, pay rate, deductions, etc.*

exemptions. There are separate tables for married and single employees — the amount of the deduction is less for those who have more exemptions. Follow the tax tables carefully to find the employee's proper federal withholding tax deduction.

If your state and city have deductions, they'll provide you with tables to figure them out. Once again, they'll probably deduct less for the employee with more exemptions, but they may not vary with marital status. Once you've computed all the deductions, add them up, subtract the total from total earnings, and you'll be left with the employee's net pay. This is the amount he'll actually receive in his paycheck.

PAYING YOUR EMPLOYEES

When you pay your employees, you should provide them with a listing of their total wages, each deduction, and net pay. You could open a separate payroll checking account. These checks come with stubs prepared for writing in this information. For a small business, however, this really isn't necessary. Simply write all the information on a piece of paper (see Figure 85), then staple the paper to the check before giving it to the employee.

You may find that most employees throw this piece of paper away and don't care how you arrived at their net pay. For those who want to keep track of their taxes and check the totals out at the end of the year, however, you should provide this information. You, of course, already have a permanent record of it in your payroll book.

Mary Sue Smith		Payroll Period Ending 3/5/74	
Gross Pay	$55.90	F.O.A.B.	$3.27
		With.	.70
	-4.27	N.Y.S.	.30
Net Pay	$51.63		$4.27

85. Rather than using a special payroll checking account, you can use a regular check and attach one of these itemized listings.

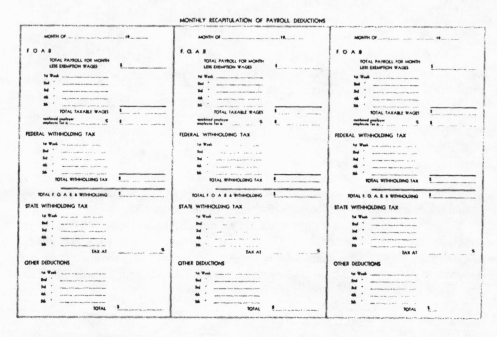

86. Recapitulations in the payroll book should be filled in at the end of each month.

MONTHLY RECAPITULATION OF DEDUCTIONS

Periods for payment of taxes are broken down yearly, quarterly, and then monthly. Depending on the amount of taxes you withhold, you'll be required to pay taxes either monthly, quarterly, or yearly. Therefore it's important to keep a monthly recapitulation of payroll deductions. In Figure 86 notice how the payroll book provides a place to make these recapitulations. Note that this page provides room for three months, or one quarter. Other books may be set up a little differently, but they'll all have a place for you to keep track of cumulative deductions of taxes.

Note that under F.O.A.B. there's a place to list "Combined Employer Employee Tax." The employee tax may be 5.85%, but the employer also contributes to F.O.A.B., so the total F.O.A.B. taxes due will be 11.7% of all employee's wages. Note also that there's a place to total F.O.A.B. and withholding taxes. This is the figure that you'll use to decide if you need to deposit these taxes monthly or quarterly.

Depositing Taxes. As explained fully in the Employer's Tax Guide, these taxes must be paid quarterly unless if at the end of any month the cumulative amount of undeposited taxes for the quarter is $200.00 or more. If the total taxes due (employee's F.O.A.B. plus employer's F.O.A.B. plus federal withholding) at the end of the first or second month are over $200.00, they must be deposited within 15 days after the end of the month.

These deposits must be made at an authorized commercial bank or a Federal Reserve Bank. Call your own bank to find out if they're qualified to take these deposits. If not, they can recommend one that is. A Federal Tax Deposit Form 501 must accompany each deposit (see Figure 87). This is sent along with a check for the amount of taxes to the commercial or Federal Reserve Bank. If your total withholding and F.I.C.A. don't accumulate to $200.00 by the end of any quarter, however, it isn't necessary to make a deposit.

87. *Form 501 should be sent with your tax deposit to an authorized commercial or Federal Reserve Bank.*

Employer's Quarterly
Federal Tax Return

SCHEDULE A—Quarterly Report of Wages Taxable under the Federal Insurance Contributions Act—FOR SOCIAL SECURITY
IF WAGES WERE NOT TAXABLE UNDER THE FICA MAKE NO ENTRIES IN ITEMS 1 THROUGH 9 AND 14 THROUGH 18

1. (First quarter only) Number of employees (except household) employed in the pay period including March 12th ►	2. Total pages of this return including this page and any pages of Form 941a ► 1	3. Total number of employees listed ► 14

List for each nonagricultural employee the WAGES taxable under the FICA which were paid during the quarter. If you pay an employee more than $10,800 in a calendar year report only the first $10,800 of such wages. In the case of "Tip Income" see instructions on page 4.

Please report each employee's name and number exactly as shown on his Social Security card.

4. EMPLOYEE'S SOCIAL SECURITY NUMBER	5. NAME OF EMPLOYEE (Please type or print)	6. TAXABLE FICA WAGES Paid to Employee in Quarter (Before deductions)		7. TAXABLE TIPS REPORTED (See page 4) If amounts in this column are not in check here □	
000 00 0000		Dollars	Cents	Dollars	Cents
231-56-0030	Judith Ambrose	252	18		
070-38-9876	Barbara Miller	394	37		
125-42-1798	David Sprague	53	28		
399-48-7891	Louise Liebherr	522	56		
088-40-5587	Rebecca Stevens	942	05		
168-38-6074	Steven Ficks	861	00		
039-26-6111	Elizabeth D'Andrea	408	50		
049-40-8827	David Hutchinson	869	50		
034-38-5882	Darcey Crandall	544	30		
137-40-6896	Elizabeth Nicholes	333	32		
173-40-0174	David Warden	941	50		
176-38-3252	Susan Campbell	35	50		
153-44-7664	John Cowan	818	30		
228-62-5702	William Wright	113	85		

If you need more space for listing employees, use Schedule A continuation sheets, Form 941a.
Totals for this page—Wage total in column 6 and tip total in column 7 ► 7070 21

8. TOTAL WAGES TAXABLE UNDER FICA PAID DURING QUARTER.
(Total of column 6 on this page and continuation sheets.) Enter here and in Item 14 below . . $ 7090.21
9. TOTAL TAXABLE TIPS REPORTED UNDER FICA DURING QUARTER. (If no tips reported, write "None.")
(Total of column 7 on this page and continuation sheets.) Enter here and in Item 15 below . . . . ► $ -

YOUR COPY

Name _____ Date Quarter Ended 12/31/73

Address _____ Employer Identification No. _____

IMPORTANT.—Keep this copy and a copy of each related schedule or statement.
Before filing the return be sure to enter on this copy your name, address,
and identification number, and the period for which the return is filed.

10. TOTAL WAGES AND TIPS SUBJECT TO WITHHOLDING PLUS OTHER COMPENSATION . . . . ►	7090	21
11. AMOUNT OF INCOME TAX WITHHELD FROM WAGES, TIPS, ANNUITIES, etc. (See instructions)	541	53
12. ADJUSTMENT FOR PRECEDING QUARTERS OF CALENDAR YEAR		
13. ADJUSTED TOTAL OF INCOME TAX WITHHELD	541	53
14. TAXABLE FICA WAGES PAID (Item 8) . . . . $ 7090.21 multiplied by 11.7% TAX	829	25
15. TAXABLE TIPS REPORTED (Item 9) . . . . $ multiplied by 5.85% TAX		
16. TOTAL FICA TAXES (Item 14 plus Item 15)	829	55
17. ADJUSTMENT (See instructions)		
18. ADJUSTED TOTAL OF FICA TAXES . . . . ►	829	55
19. TOTAL TAXES (Item 13 plus Item 18)	1371	08
20. TOTAL DEPOSITS FOR QUARTER (INCLUDING FINAL DEPOSIT MADE FOR QUARTER) AND OVERPAYMENT FROM PREVIOUS QUARTER LIST IN SCHEDULE B (See instructions on page 4)	1371	08

Note: If undeposited taxes at the end of the quarter are $200 or more, the full amount must be deposited with
an authorized commercial bank or a Federal Reserve bank. This deposit must be entered in Schedule B
and included in Item 20.

21. UNDEPOSITED TAXES DUE (ITEM 19 minus ITEM 20—THIS SHOULD BE LESS THAN $200). PAY TO INTERNAL REVENUE SERVICE AND ENTER HERE	0	

22. IF ITEM 20 IS MORE THAN ITEM 19, ENTER EXCESS HERE ► $ _____ AND CHECK IF YOU WANT IT □ APPLIED TO NEXT RETURN, OR □ REFUNDED.

23. If not liable for returns in succeeding quarters write "FINAL" here ► _____ and enter date of final payment of taxable wages here ► _____
SEE "WHERE TO FILE" ON PAGE 2.

*88. Form 941 is to be filled out quarterly and sent to the I.R.S. along with any
unpaid taxes.*

FORM 941

At the end of each quarter you're required to fill out Form 941, listing names of employees, social security numbers, taxable F.I.C.A. wages, withholding taxes, and totals. When you send in the form (which is due before the last day of the following month), you must send with it a check for any taxes that weren't deposited at an authorized commercial or Federal Reserve Bank.

In a sample Form 941 (see Figure 88), note that you must list each employee and his total taxable F.I.C.A. wages before deductions. Since no tips were paid, this column is left blank. On Line 14, the taxable F.I.C.A. wages paid are multiplied by 11.7%, which is the combined amount paid by employees and employer. This is added to the total income tax withheld on Line 13 to get the total taxes on Line 19. Since all these taxes had already been deposited at a commercial bank, there were no undeposited taxes due.

FEDERAL UNEMPLOYMENT TAX

Federal unemployment tax is required to be paid on or before every January 31st for the preceding year. Form 940 (see Figure 89) must be filled in and the balance due (on Line 18) must be sent in along with the form. If your quarterly unemployment taxes amount to more than $100, they must be deposited quarterly.

Note that this federal unemployment tax is paid by the employer, not deducted from the employee's wages. There's also a provision whereby if you pay state unemployment taxes, part of these may be deducted from the federal unemployment taxes you'd otherwise pay. On the sample shown, $405.86 was paid in New York State unemployment taxes. We were allowed to deduct $306.97 of this from the gross federal tax (Line 14) so the final balance due the Internal Revenue Service was $65.94. Detailed instructions are given on the back of Form 940. Read these carefully, then check with your state unemployment insurance agency if you have one to make sure you're filing correctly.

STATE AND CITY TAXES

Your state and city agencies will provide you with information booklets and forms telling you to compute and deduct taxes, when to make deposits and send in forms, etc. The important thing is to tell them right away that you're a new employer so you get the information on time. Then read the instructions and mark your calendar to remind yourself when these forms and payments are due.

Usually, with only a few employees, you'll find that you don't have to file state forms as often. As in the federal taxes, it depends on the dollar amount withheld. The more taxes withheld, the more often you're required to deposit them. Most tax forms are filed on a quarterly basis. Make sure you take the proper deductions from each employee's wages because you'll be responsible for paying them whether you deduct or not.

FORM W-2

At the end of the year you'll be required to provide every person employed by you during the previous year with a W-2 Form listing total wages and taxes deducted for the whole year. These must be given to employees not later than January 31st of the following year. If, however, an employee leaves before the end of the year and you don't expect

Employer's Annual Federal Unemployment Tax Return

1973

Schedule A—Computation of Credit Against Federal Unemployment Tax

Name of State (1)	State reporting number as shown on employer's State contribution returns (2)	Taxable payroll (As defined in State act) (3)	Experience rate period (4)		Experi- ence rate (5)	Contributions had rate been 2.7% (col. 3 × 2.7%) (6)	Contributions payable at experience rate (col. 3 × col. 5) (7)	Additional credit (col. 6 minus col. 7) (8)	Contributions actually paid to State (9)
			From—	To—					
N.Y		11274							405.86
	Totals ▶	11274							

10. Total tentative credit (Column 8 plus column 9) 405.86
11. Enter 2.7% of the amount of wages shown in Item 13 below 306.97
12. Credit allowable (Item 10 or 11 whichever is smaller). Enter here and in Item 15 . . . .   306.97

KEEP THIS COPY
FOR YOUR RECORDS

You must retain this copy, and a copy of each related schedule or statement for a period of 4 years after the date the tax is due or paid, whichever is the later. These copies must be available for inspection by the Internal Revenue Service.

Calendar Year
1973
Identification No.

Calendar Year
1973
Identification No.

13. Total taxable wages paid during calendar year (From Schedule B, on other side) . . . .   11369 : 25

14. Gross Federal tax (3.28% of Item 13) . . . .   372 : 91

15. Less: Credit (State taxes paid and additional credit) from Item 12, Schedule A . . . .   306 : 97

16. Item 14 less Item 15 . . . .   65 : 94

17. Total Federal tax deposited (From Schedule C, on other side)   0

18. Balance Due (Item 16 less Item 17). Pay to "Internal Revenue Service" . . . . ▶   65 : 94
19. If no longer in business at end of year, write "FINAL" here ▶

Important.—Before filing the return be sure to enter on this copy your name, address, and identification number.

89. Form 940 is for reporting federal unemployment taxes at the end of each year and must be filed on or before January 31.

him to return within that year, the statement should be given to him within 30 days after his last wages were paid.

In Figure 90, a sample W-2 Form, Item 1 is the total federal income tax withheld for the year. Item 2 lists total wages paid. Item 3 lists F.I.C.A. or social security withheld (note that this figure is the amount withheld from the employee, not the total paid by employee and employer). Item 4 lists the total F.I.C.A. wages, which in most cases will be the same as Item 2. Items 6, 7, and 8 are provided for state or local income tax information. (Your state and local government will probably provide you with their own forms for this purpose, however.)

Other information listed on the form is the employee's name and address, his social security number, and his marital status. At the top of the form, type in the company name and address and employer's identifying number. These W-2 Forms come in sets, with copies for the employer, the employee, the federal government, the state government, for the employee to file with his federal and state tax forms.

A W-3 Transmittal Form is used to transmit the federal Internal Revenue Service copies to them (see Figure 91). Detailed instructions on filling out these forms are provided in the government instruction booklets you'll receive.

FORM 1099-MISC.

If you pay sales commissions to sales representatives, or any other monies that don't have taxes deducted from them, these payments should be reported on Form 1099-Misc. (see Figure 92). Sales commissions are listed under Item 3, "Commissions and Fees To Nonemployees." This form also comes with several copies, as does the W-2 Form. Send a set to each of your sales representatives before January 31st of the following year in which they earned commissions.

Copy A for the Internal Revenue Service Center should be sent with a transmittal slip, Form 1096 (see Figure 93). Note that we've put an "X" in the box marked "Without Taxpayer Identifying No." because our 1099 Forms don't list the sales reps' identifying social security numbers.

PAYROLL TAX SUMMARY

As soon as you hire your first employee you'll be liable for withholding federal withholding and social security from his salary, and depositing and reporting these taxes to the Internal Revenue Service. You'll also be liable for federal unemployment taxes and paying your employer's share of social security. You may also be liable for state and local withholding and unemployment taxes. In addition, you'll probably have to get some kind of workman's compensation and disability insurance.

Find out about your tax responsibilities early and set up your records to handle them. Mark your calendar at least five days in advance of each deposit and filing due date to give yourself time to prepare the forms. If you have any problems, or don't understand exactly what your responsibilities are, call your local agencies. They'll be glad to help you out. Remember, it's illegal not to deduct taxes. If you don't, and you're found out at a later date, you'll be legally responsible for paying them, plus fines for lateness.

90. *A W-2 Form should be sent to each employee listing earnings and deductions from the previous year.*

91. *This W-3 Transmittal Form is used to send I.R.S. copies of all W-2 Forms.*

HOLY COW LEATHER
180 Horton Rd.
Newfield, N.Y. 14867   16-1010633

Copy C
For Payer

Type or print PAYER'S Federal identifying number, name, address and ZIP code above.

1	Rents	2	Royalties	3	Commissions and fees to nonemployees (No Form W-2 items)	4	Prizes and awards to nonemployees (No Form W-2 items)	5	Other fixed or determinable income (Specify)
					$747.81				

RECIPIENT'S Identifying number ▶

Sam G. Armstrong
310 Engleman Ave.
Burlington, N.C. 27215

Type or print RECIPIENT'S name, address and ZIP code above.

An "X" in the upper left corner indicates this is a corrected form.

Form **1099-MISC**

Department of the Treasury—Internal Revenue Service

92. A 1099-Misc. Form such as this should be sent to sales reps listing commissions earned the previous year.

Form **1096**

Annual Summary and Transmittal of U.S. Information Returns

1973

Department of the Treasury
Internal Revenue Service

(Magnetic tape filers: See the applicable Revenue Procedures regarding transmittal of returns on magnetic tape.)

Enter number of documents	Place an "X" in the proper box to identify type of document being transmitted				All documents are: Place an "X" in the proper boxes. (See instructions.)			
					Original	Corrected	With taxpayer identifying no.	Without taxpayer identifying no.
11	1099–DIV	1099–INT	1099–MED	1099–MISC X	X			X
	1099–OID	1099–L	1099–PATR	1087–DIV				
	1087–INT	1087–MED	1087–MISC	1087–OID				

PAYER'S identifying number ▶ *16-1010633*

Holy Cow Leather
180 Horton Rd.
Newfield, N.Y. 14867

Type or print PAYER'S name, address and ZIP code above.

Under penalties of perjury, I declare that I have examined this return, including accompanying documents and to the best of my knowledge and belief, it is true, correct, and complete. In the case of documents without recipients' identifying numbers I have complied with the requirements of the law by requesting such numbers from the recipients, but did not receive them.

Signature _____ Title *Owner* _____ Date *1/21/74*

☆ U.S. GOVERNMENT PRINTING OFFICE:1973—O-458-087   E.I. 25-1118272

93. This 1906 Transmittal Form is used to send the I.R.S. copies of 1099-Misc. Forms.

CHECKLIST

1. Register as an employer with Internal Revenue Service and your state and local tax agencies. Ask for forms and information.

2. Each new employee must fill out a W-4 or W-4E Form on or before their first day of employment.

3. Check your state laws on Workmen's Compensation and Disability Insurance. Ask your local agency or your insurance agency for information.

4. Get a payroll book and keep employee time, wages, deductions, etc., in it.

5. Use the tax guides for computing taxes. Federal withholding taxes are based on marital status and number of exemptions. Social Security is a flat percentage. State and local withholding taxes may be based strictly on number of exemptions.

6. When you pay your employees, provide them with a list of their gross pay, deductions, and net pay.

7. At the end of each month do a recapitulation of total taxes in your payroll book. Depending on the total federal withholding and social security taxes, you may have to make a deposit in an authorized commercial or Federal Reserve Bank at this time.

8. At the end of each quarter you're required to fill in a Form 941, listing employees, social security numbers, taxable wages, withholding taxes, and totals. This form is due before the last day of the following month. At this time you must send with it a check for any taxes that weren't previously deposited at an authorized commercial or Federal Reserve Bank.

9. Federal unemployment tax must be paid on or before every January 31st for the preceding year. Use Form 940 for reporting. If your quarterly unemployment taxes amount to more than $100.00, they must be deposited quarterly.

10. Follow procedures outlined by state and local tax agencies for filing reports and paying state and local withholding and unemployment taxes.

11. By January 31st of each following year, you're required to give employees W-2 Forms listing their wages and taxes for the previous year. Use a W-3 Transmittal Form to transmit copies to Internal Revenue Service.

12. For any payments, such as commissions to sales reps, where no tax deductions were made, send each rep a Form 1099 Misc., listing payments. Use a Form 1096 for transmittal to Internal Revenue Service.

17

FEDERAL INCOME TAXES

If your business is a proprietorship or partnership, business profit will be considered part of your personal earnings. You'll still fill out the regular Form 1040 Individual Income Tax Return. Business profit will be added to any other income of yours (if joint account, yours and your spouse's), and losses from the business should be subtracted from any other income. If your business is making a profit, Form 1040-ES, a Declaration of Estimated Tax for Individuals, should be filed quarterly. If the profit from your business is your only income, you should also file a Schedule SE for Computation of Social Security Self-Employment Tax. To show the profit or loss your business made, a Schedule C, which lists business income and deductions, should be attached to your Form 1040. We'll go over each of these items in detail. The important thing is, whether the business has a profit or loss, it's added or subtracted from any other income you may have. No federal income taxes are paid separately on the business.

PROFIT OR LOSS

In Chapter 7 we discussed yearly income statements. The profit or loss from this income statement should match the profit or loss you show on your federal income tax return. All operating costs and other business expenses are allowable business deductions. If your yearly income statement indicates your sales for the year were greater than business expenses, you'll show a profit. If your expenses were greater than sales, or revenues, you'll show a loss.

SCHEDULE C – CASH BASIS

Schedule C is the form you should fill out to show "Profit (or Loss) from Business or Profession," and attach to your Form 1040. In general, Schedule C should reflect the profit or loss as indicated on your income statement for the year. When your business is new and small, you may be operating on a strictly cash basis – profit equals money taken in minus money spent. This is especially true if you only accepted cash from individuals at craft fairs, etc., and had no inventory or major equipment to speak of.

Figures 94 and 95 illustrate the front and back of Schedule C filled out for a simple business operation with no inventory, no equipment to depreciate, and goods sold on a cash basis only (no accounts receivable). We also assumed this business had no employees, and didn't pay commissions, etc. It's simply a small, one-person operation selling directly to individuals and at craft fairs.

FORM 1040

The net profit or loss on Line 21 of Schedule C should be entered on Line 28, Part I of Form 1040, "Business Income or (Loss)." This is added to other income, if any, in Lines 29 through 37, then totaled and entered on Line 12 on the front of Form 1040. If you have a business loss, and either you or your spouse was employed that year, the business loss will offset your other income and you'll probably receive a substantial refund on income taxes deducted from your salaries.

For example, suppose you earned $10,000 in salary from a regular job and had $2,000 deducted in taxes. Your business loss of, say, $4,000 would lower your total gross income to $6,000. Taxes on $6,000 would be less than what you paid on $10,000. Therefore you'd be entitled to a refund. Sometimes a new business won't show a profit the first year of its operation, or longer. But at least you can deduct these losses from your total income.

If you have no other income but the business and it shows a loss one year, you can apply this loss to future years. Read your I.R.S. instruction booklet to find out how this works.

SCHEDULE C – ACCRUAL BASIS

If your business accounting kept track of beginning and ending inventories, accounts receivable and payable, then you should use the "accrual" method for filling out Schedule C. This means you report income when earned, even if not received, and deduct expenses when incurred, even if not paid during that tax year. We'll use the yearly income statement as shown in Figure 48, Chapter 7, to illustrate how to transfer these figures to Schedule C (see Figures 96 and 97).

SCHEDULE C – BACK (PAGE 2)

We'll start with Figure 97, Schedule C-1, "Cost of Goods Sold and/or Operations." Line 1 is $3,000, figured by adding Finished Goods Inventory 1/1/74 of $500.00 to Raw Materials Inventory 1/1/74 of $2,500. Line 2 is left blank since this business is strictly manufacturing. No finished goods purchases were made. If the operation were a retail store, inventory would include store inventory and purchases would be wholesale items purchased for resale.

Line 3 is $10,000, taken directly from "Salaries" on the income statement. Line 4, "Materials and Supplies," is $15,000, taken directly from "Basic Materials" on the income statement. Line 5, "Other Costs," is $5,500, figured by adding $500.00 freight and $5,000 tools and equipment. A separate sheet should be attached showing this breakdown.

Line 6 is the total of Lines 1 through 5. On Line 7, the ending inventory, "Finished Goods and Raw Materials," or $1,300, is listed. This ending inventory is subtracted from Line 6 to give Line 8 $32,200.

Note that the method of inventory evaluation listed is "cost." I.R.S. instructions state that "inventories can be valued at: (1) cost, (2) cost or market, whichever is is lower, or (3) any other method approved by the Commissioner." For more details on inventory evaluation, see the accounting book listed in the appendix.

The only other area we're concerned with on page 2 is Schedule C-4, "Expense Account Information." The owner of the business spent $320.00 in expenses on sales trips, interviewing sales representatives, etc.

SCHEDULE C – FRONT (PAGE 1)

Lines A through J are self-explanatory. On Line 1, list gross receipts or sales, $50,000. Discounts of $200.00 are considered allowances. These are deducted from sales to get the balance of $49,800. On Line 2, copy your cost of goods sold from Line 8 on Schedule C-1, page 2. Subtract Line 2 from Line 1 to get gross profit of $17,600. Since there was no other business income, this line is left blank. Line 5 is the same as Line 3.

Now the rest of the business expenses on the income statement must be listed. Rent of $1,200 is covered on Line 8. Sales commissions are listed on Line 13. Bad debts go on Line 17. "Office Supplies and Miscellaneous Expenses" are left. These are listed under Line 19, "Other Business Expenses." Since $320.00 of the total $800.00 miscellaneous expenses were owner's business expenses, these are listed separately here and on Schedule C-4 on page 2 as shown above.

Line 20 is the total deductions from Lines 6 through 19. Subtract this total from Line 5 to get "Net Profit." This amount should be entered on Line 28, Form 1040. This income will be added to any other income and taxed in the same manner as any other personal income.

DEPRECIATION

If any of your business purchases during the year were major equipment expected to last for several years, these items can't be deducted fully as expenses the year they were purchased. You're only allowed to deduct a fraction or part of the total cost each year.

See Figure 98, Schedule C-2, for an example showing how to list depreciation of machinery and other equipment on your income tax return. A company bought a machine that cost $1,000 and was expected to be useful for five years. They used the straight-line method of depreciation, which means they divide the total life of the machine, five, into the cost, $1,000, to get the depreciation cost per year of $200.00 Note that if the machine had been purchased in the middle of the year, and let's say used for six months, only $100.00 would be allowed in depreciation costs for that year.

There are other methods of computing depreciation. Some of them allow larger amounts to be applied to the initial years of useful life, thus giving a tax advantage at this time. For more information on methods of computing depreciation, ask your I.R.S. office for Form 4562 and Publication 534. These will give you all the accepted I.R.S. methods, limitations, and special rules. The basic accounting book listed in the appendix will also give you detailed information on various depreciation computation methods and how they apply to your over-all bookkeeping system.

Profit (or Loss) From Business or Profession
(Sole Proprietorship)

► Attach to Form 1040.
► Partnerships, joint ventures, etc., must file Form 1065.

1972

Name(s) as shown on Form 1040

Social security number

A Principal business activity.......... Retail ....; product .... Crafts ....
(See Schedule C Instructions)   (For example: retail—hardware; wholesale—tobacco; services—legal; manufacturing—furniture; etc.)

B Business name .... **C** Employer Identification Number ....

D Business address (number and street) ....

City, State and ZIP code ....

E Indicate method of accounting: (1) ☒ cash; (2) ☐ accrual; (3) ☐ other.

F Were you required to file Form 1096 for 1972? (See Schedule C Instructions) ☐ YES ☒ NO. If "Yes," where filed? ► ....

G Is this business located within the boundaries of the city, town, etc., indicated? ☒ YES ☐ NO.

H Did you own this business at the end of 1972? ☐ YES ☒ NO.

I How many months in 1972 did you own this business? ....8....

J Was an Employer's Quarterly Federal Tax Return, Form 941, filed for this business for any quarter in 1972? ☐ YES ☒ NO.

IMPORTANT—All applicable lines and schedules must be filled in.

INCOME

1	Gross receipts or sales $10,000 .... Less returns and allowances $.......... Balance ►	10,000
2	Less: Cost of goods sold and/or operations (Schedule C–1, line 8)	4,000
3	Gross profit	6,000
4	Other income (attach schedule)	
5	TOTAL income (add lines 3 and 4)	6,000

DEDUCTIONS

6	Depreciation (explain in Schedule C–2)		
7	Taxes on business and business property (explain in Schedule C–3)		
8	Rent on business property		600
9	Repairs (explain in Schedule C–3)		
10	Salaries and wages not included on line 3, Schedule C–1 (exclude any paid to yourself)		
11	Insurance		
12	Legal and professional fees		
13	Commissions		
14	Amortization (attach statement)		
15	(a) Pension and profit-sharing plans (see Schedule C Instructions)		
	(b) Employee benefit programs (see Schedule C Instructions)		
16	Interest on business indebtedness		
17	Bad debts arising from sales or services		
18	Depletion		
19	Other business expenses (specify):		
	(a) Show fees	250	
	(b) Expenses during show	750	
	(c)		
	(d)		
	(e)		
	(f)		
	(g)		
	(h)		
	(i)		
	(j)		
	(k)		
	(l)		
	(m)		
	(n)		
	(o)		
	(p) Total other business expenses (add lines 19(a) through 19(o))		1,000
20	Total deductions (add lines 6 through 19)		1,600
21	Net profit (or loss) (subtract line 20 from line 5). Enter here and on line 35, Form 1040. ALSO enter on Schedule SE, line 1		4,400

94. The front of Schedule C when you use a cash basis bookkeeping system.

SCHEDULE C–1. COST OF GOODS SOLD AND/OR OPERATIONS (See Schedule C Instructions for line 2)

1 Inventory at beginning of year (if different from last year's closing inventory, attach explanation) . . . . .

2 Purchases $..................................... Less cost of items withdrawn for personal use $....................... Balance ▶

3 Cost of labor (do not include salary paid to yourself) . . . .

4 Materials and supplies . . . .   4,000 | 00

5 Other costs (attach schedule) . . . .

6 Total of lines 1 through 5 . . . .   4,000 | 00

7 Less: Inventory at end of year . . . .

8 Cost of goods sold and/or operations. Enter here and on line 2, page 1. . . . .   4,000 | 00

Method of inventory valuation ▶

Was there any substantial change in the manner of determining quantities, costs, or valuations between the opening and closing inventories? ☐ YES ☐ NO. If "Yes," attach explanation.

SCHEDULE C–2. DEPRECIATION (See Schedule C Instructions for line 6)

Note: If depreciation is computed by using the Class Life (ADR) System for assets placed in service after December 31, 1970, or the Guideline Class Life System for assets placed in service before January 1, 1971, you must file Form 4832 (Class Life (ADR) System) or Form 5006 (Guideline Class Life System). Except as otherwise expressly provided in income tax regulations sections 1.167(a)–11(b)(5)(vi) and 1.167(a)–12, the provisions of Revenue Procedures 62–21 and 65–13 are not applicable for taxable years ending after December 31, 1970, If you need more space, use Form 4562.

Check box if you made an election this taxable year to use ☐ Class Life (ADR) System and/or ☐ Guideline Class Life System.

a. Group and guideline class or description of property	b. Date acquired	c. Cost or other basis	d. Depreciation allowed or allowable in prior years	e. Method of computing depreciation	f. Life or rate	g. Depreciation for this year
1 Total additional first-year depreciation (do not include in items below)			➔			
2 Depreciation from Form 4832						
3 Depreciation from Form 5006						
4 Other depreciation:						
Buildings						
Furniture and fixtures						
Transportation equipment . . .						
Machinery and other equipment .						
Other (specify)						
5 Totals						
6 Less amount of depreciation claimed in Schedule C–1						
7 Balance—Enter here and on page 1, line 6						

SUMMARY OF DEPRECIATION (Other Than Additional First Year Depreciation)

	Straight line	Declining balance	Sum of the years-digits	Units of production	Other (specify)	Total
1 Depreciation from Form 4832 . .						
2 Depreciation from Form 5006 . .						
3 Other . . .						

SCHEDULE C–3. EXPLANATION OF LINES 7 AND 9

Line No.	Explanation	Amount	Line No.	Explanation	Amount
		$			$

SCHEDULE C–4. EXPENSE ACCOUNT INFORMATION (See Schedule C Instructions for Schedule C–4)

Enter information with regard to yourself and your five highest paid employees. In determining the five highest paid employees, expense account allowances must be added to their salaries and wages. However, the information need not be submitted for any employee for whom the combined amount is less than $10,000, or for yourself if your expense account allowance plus line 21, page 1, is less than $10,000.

	Name	Expense account	Salaries and Wages
Owner			
1			
2			
3			
4			
5			

Did you claim a deduction for expenses connected with:

(1) Entertainment facility (boat, resort, ranch, etc.)? . . ☐ YES ☐ NO   (3) Employees' families at conventions or meetings? . . . ☐ YES ☐ NO

(2) Living accommodations (except employees on business)? ☐ YES ☐ NO   (4) Employee or family vacations not reported on Form W–2? ☐ YES ☐ NO

95. Here is the back of Schedule C filled out for a cash basis system.

Profit (or Loss) From Business or Profession
(Sole Proprietorship)
▶ Attach to Form 1040.
▶ Partnerships, joint ventures, etc., must file Form 1065.

1972

Name(s) as shown on Form 1040 | Social security number

A Principal business activity ____wholesale____ ; product ____leather accessories____
(See Schedule C Instructions) (For example: retail—hardware; wholesale—tobacco; services—legal; manufacturing—furniture; etc.)

B Business name .... **C** Employer Identification Number __16__ __-253400__

D Business address (number and street) ....

City, State and ZIP code ....

E Indicate method of accounting: (1) ☐ cash; (2) ☒ accrual; (3) ☐ other.

F Were you required to file Form 1096 for 1972? (See Schedule C Instructions) ☒ YES ☐ NO. If "Yes," where filed? ▶ ....

G Is this business located within the boundaries of the city, town, etc., indicated? ☒ YES ☐ NO.

H Did you own this business at the end of 1972? ☒ YES ☐ NO.

I How many months in 1972 did you own this business? __12__

J Was an Employer's Quarterly Federal Tax Return, Form 941, filed for this business for any quarter in 1972? ☒ YES ☐ NO.

IMPORTANT—All applicable lines and schedules must be filled in.

	INCOME		
1	Gross receipts or sales $ 50,000 Less returns and allowances $ 200 Balance ▶		49,800
2	Less: Cost of goods sold and/or operations (Schedule C–1, line 8)		32,200
3	Gross profit		17,600
4	Other income (attach schedule)		—
5	TOTAL income (add lines 3 and 4)		17,600

	DEDUCTIONS		
6	Depreciation (explain in Schedule C–2)		—
7	Taxes on business and business property (explain in Schedule C–3)		—
8	Rent on business property		1,200
9	Repairs (explain in Schedule C–3)		—
10	Salaries and wages not included on line 3, Schedule C–1 (exclude any paid to yourself) .		—
11	Insurance		—
12	Legal and professional fees		—
13	Commissions		3,000
14	Amortization (attach statement)		—
15	(a) Pension and profit-sharing plans (see Schedule C Instructions)		—
	(b) Employee benefit programs (see Schedule C Instructions)		—
16	Interest on business indebtedness		—
17	Bad debts arising from sales or services		100
18	Depletion		—
19	Other business expenses (specify):		
	(a) Office Supplies	300	
	(b) Expense Account - Owner	320	
	(c) Misc. Expenses	480	
	(d)		
	(e)		
	(f)		
	(g)		
	(h)		
	(i)		
	(j)		
	(k)		
	(l)		
	(m)		
	(n)		
	(o)		
	(p) Total other business expenses (add lines 19(a) through 19(o))		1,100
20	Total deductions (add lines 6 through 19)		5,400
21	Net profit (or loss) (subtract line 20 from line 5). Enter here and on line 35, Form 1040. ALSO enter on Schedule SE, line 1		12,200

96. The front of Schedule C illustrating an accrual system of bookkeeping.

SCHEDULE C–1. COST OF GOODS SOLD AND/OR OPERATIONS (See Schedule C Instructions for line 2)

1 Inventory at beginning of year (if different from last year's closing inventory, attach explanation) . . . . . . | 3,000
2 Purchases $.................................. Less cost of items withdrawn for personal use $.................................. Balance ▶ | —
3 Cost of labor (do not include salary paid to yourself) . . . . | 10,000
4 Materials and supplies . . . . | 15,000
5 Other costs (attach schedule) . . . . | 5,500
6 Total of lines 1 through 5 . . . . | 33,500
7 Less: Inventory at end of year . . . . | 1,300
8 Cost of goods sold and/or operations. Enter here and on line 2, page 1. . . . . | 32,200

Method of inventory valuation ▶ _COST_

Was there any substantial change in the manner of determining quantities, costs, or valuation's between the opening and closing inventories? ☐ YES ☒ NO. If "Yes," attach explanation.

SCHEDULE C–2. DEPRECIATION (See Schedule C Instructions for line 6)

Note: If depreciation is computed by using the Class Life (ADR) System for assets placed in service after December 31, 1970, or the Guideline Class Life System for assets placed in service before January 1, 1971, you must file Form 4832 (Class Life (ADR) System) or Form 5006 (Guideline Class Life System). Except as otherwise expressly provided in income tax regulations sections 1.167(a)–11(b)(5)(vi) and 1.167(a)–12, the provisions of Revenue Procedures 62–21 and 65–13 are not applicable for taxable years ending after December 31, 1970. If you need more space, use Form 4562.

Check box if you made an election this taxable year to use ☐ Class Life (ADR) System and/or ☐ Guideline Class Life System.

a. Group and guideline class or description of property	b. Date acquired	c. Cost or other basis	d. Depreciation allowed or allowable in prior years	e. Method of computing depreciation	f. Life or rate	g. Depreciation for this year
1 Total additional first-year depreciation (do not include in items below) ▶						
2 Depreciation from Form 4832			/////	/////	/////	
3 Depreciation from Form 5006			/////	/////	/////	
4 Other depreciation:						
Buildings						
Furniture and fixtures						
Transportation equipment . . .						
Machinery and other equipment .						
Other (specify)_____						
_____						
_____						
_____						
5 Totals						
6 Less amount of depreciation claimed in Schedule C–1						
7 Balance—Enter here and on page 1, line 6						

SUMMARY OF DEPRECIATION (Other Than Additional First Year Depreciation)

	Straight line	Declining balance	Sum of the years-digits	Units of production	Other (specify)	Total
1 Depreciation from Form 4832 . .				/////	/////	
2 Depreciation from Form 5006 . .				/////	/////	
3 Other . . .						

SCHEDULE C–3. EXPLANATION OF LINES 7 AND 9

Line No.	Explanation	Amount	Line No.	Explanation	Amount
		$			$

SCHEDULE C–4. EXPENSE ACCOUNT INFORMATION (See Schedule C Instructions for Schedule C–4)

Enter information with regard to yourself and your five highest paid employees. In determining the five highest paid employees, expense account allowances must be added to their salaries and wages. However, the information need not be submitted for any employee for whom the combined amount is less than $10,000, or for yourself if your expense account allowance plus line 21, page 1, is less than $10,000.

	Name	Expense account	Salaries and Wages
Owner		320.00	/////
1			
2			
3			
4			
5			

Did you claim a deduction for expenses connected with:

(1) Entertainment facility (boat, resort, ranch, etc.)? . . ☐ YES ☐ NO (3) Employees' families at conventions or meetings? . . . ☐ YES ☐ NO
(2) Living accommodations (except employees on business)? ☐ YES ☐ NO (4) Employee or family vacations not reported on Form W–2? ☐ YES ☐ NO

☆☆☆☆ U.S. GOVERNMENT PRINTING OFFICE:1972—O–458-277

E.I. 13-8687300

97. *The back of Schedule C filled out according to the accrual system.*

SCHEDULE C–1. COST OF GOODS SOLD AND/OR OPERATIONS (See Schedule C Instructions for line 2)

1 Inventory at beginning of year (if different from last year's closing inventory, attach explanation)	
2 Purchases $................................. Less cost of items withdrawn for personal use $.................................... Balance ▶	
3 Cost of labor (do not include salary paid to yourself)	
4 Materials and supplies	
5 Other costs (attach schedule)	
6 Total of lines 1 through 5	
7 Less: Inventory at end of year	
8 Cost of goods sold and/or operations. Enter here and on line 2, page 1.	

Method of inventory valuation ▶

Was there any substantial change in the manner of determining quantities, costs, or valuations between the opening and closing inventories? ☐ YES ☐ NO. If "Yes," attach explanation.

SCHEDULE C–2. DEPRECIATION (See Schedule C Instructions for line 6)

Note: If depreciation is computed by using the Class Life (ADR) System for assets placed in service after December 31, 1970, or the Guideline Class Life System for assets placed in service before January 1, 1971, you must file Form 4832 (Class Life (ADR) System) or Form 5006 (Guideline Class Life System). Except as otherwise expressly provided in income tax regulations sections 1.167(a)–11(b)(5)(vi) and 1.167(a)–12, the provisions of Revenue Procedures 62–21 and 65–13 are not applicable for taxable years ending after December 31, 1970. If you need more space, use Form 4832.

Check box if you made an election this taxable year to use ☐ Class Life (ADR) System and/or ☐ Guideline Class Life System.

a. Group and guideline class or description of property	b. Date acquired	c. Cost or other basis	d. Depreciation allowed or allowable in prior years	e. Method of computing depreciation	f. Life or rate	g. Depreciation for this year
1 Total additional first-year depreciation (do not include in items below) ——————————▶						
2 Depreciation from Form 4832			/////	/////	/////	
3 Depreciation from Form 5006			/////	/////	/////	
4 Other depreciation:						
Buildings						
Furniture and fixtures						
Transportation equipment . . .						
Machinery and other equipment .	1/5/73	1,000	—	Straight-line	5 yrs.	200
Other (specify)_____						
5 Totals		1,000	. . . . . .			200
6 Less amount of depreciation claimed in Schedule C–1						—
7 Balance—Enter here and on page 1, line 6						200

SUMMARY OF DEPRECIATION (Other Than Additional First Year Depreciation)

	Straight line	Declining balance	Sum of the years-digits	Units of production	Other (specify)	Total
1 Depreciation from Form 4832 . .				/////	/////	
2 Depreciation from Form 5006 . .						
3 Other . . .						

SCHEDULE C–3. EXPLANATION OF LINES 7 AND 9

Line No.	Explanation	Amount	Line No.	Explanation	Amount
		$			$

SCHEDULE C–4. EXPENSE ACCOUNT INFORMATION (See Schedule C Instructions for Schedule C–4)

Enter information with regard to yourself and your five highest paid employees. In determining the five highest paid employees, expense account allowances must be added to their salaries and wages. However, the information need not be submitted for any employee for whom the combined amount is less than $10,000, or for yourself if your expense account allowance plus line 21, page 1, is less than $10,000.

	Name	Expense account	Salaries and Wages
Owner			/////
1			
2			
3			
4			
5			

Did you claim a deduction for expenses connected with:

(1) Entertainment facility (boat, resort, ranch, etc.)? . . ☐ YES ☐ NO   (3) Employees' families at conventions or meetings? . . . ☐ YES ☐ NO

(2) Living accommodations (except employees on business)? ☐ YES ☐ NO   (4) Employee or family vacations not reported on Form W–2? ☐ YES ☐ NO

☆☆☆☆ U.S. GOVERNMENT PRINTING OFFICE: 1972—O–456–277   R.I. 13-3687290

98. *Schedule C-2 from the back of Schedule C, illustrates how to account for depreciation on major machinery and equipment purchases.*

SELF-EMPLOYMENT TAXES

Schedule SE is for "Computation of Social Security Self-Employment Tax." If you earned wages of $10,800 or more that were subject to social security taxes, there's no need to fill in this form. The maximum salary anyone paid social security on in 1973 was $10,800. This figure will undoubtedly rise in years to come.

The point is, if you already had social security taxes deducted from this amount of wages, you don't have to pay any more. If, however, your sole income was from self-employment, or a combination whereby you earned less than the specified $10,800 at another job, then you may be eligible to file Schedule SE. If your total self-employment income was *less* than $400.00, however, you're not subject to self-employment tax.

See Figures 99 and 100 for examples of a Schedule SE form filled out. We've used the net income from the Schedule C in Figures 96 and 97, $12,200. Since this amount was the sole income for this person, the form is simple to fill out. As the form instructs, since there was only non-farm income, only Parts II and III must be filled out.

In Figure 99 the net income, $12,200, is entered on Line (a) Part II. Since there was no other income, Lines 6 and 8 are the same. This figure is transferred to Line 12 (b) on Part III (see Figure 100). Since there were no F.I.C.A. or other wages earned, Lines 15 (a) and (b) are left blank. This 0 amount is subtracted from Line 14, to get $10,800. Line 17 is the self-employment income, either $10,800 (the maximum) or Line 13 (total net earnings), whichever is smaller. In this case, the person was required to pay the 8% tax on the $10,800, or $864.00. This amount should then be entered on Form 1040, Line 55. It will be added to total taxes owed. For more detailed information on self-employment tax, ask your I.R.S. office for Publication 533.

ESTIMATED TAXES

If you expect to make a profit on your business for the following year, you're supposed to pay taxes on this income by April 15th of that year or in four equal installments. If, however, the tax you'd expect to owe was under $100.00, you wouldn't be required to do this.

As a new business it may be very tough to figure out whether you'll make a profit the following year, and how much that loss or gain might be. We suggest you wait until you actually start making a profit. For example, suppose you start a business in February. It starts making a profit in August of the same year. You can then file a 1040-ES "Declaration of Estimated Tax for Individuals" by September 15th for the last quarter.

Once you've had some experience, it will be easier to estimate your earnings. If you find that each year, for example, your earnings tend to increase by 10%, you can use this information in estimating future income. If you're not accurate, however, adjustments can be made with each quarterly declaration voucher.

Figure 101 shows the 1073 Estimated Tax Worksheet and the first quarterly Form 1040-ES Voucher. The worksheet allows you to compute your estimated tax based on earnings, exemptions, deductions, etc. It provides a place for you to record your estimated tax payments. It also provides a space for you to work out an amended computation if your situation changes during the year. Full instructions and tax tables are printed on the reverse side of Form 1040-ES. You can also get Publication 421, Optional Self-Employment Tax Table, from I.R.S.

Computation of Social Security Self-Employment Tax

► Each self-employed person must file a Schedule SE.
► Attach to Form 1040.

1973

- If you had wages, including tips, of $10,800 or more that were subject to social security taxes, do not fill in this form.
- If you had more than one business, combine profits and losses from all your businesses and farms on this Schedule SE.

Important.—The self-employment income reported below will be credited to your social security record and used in figuring social security benefits.

NAME OF SELF-EMPLOYED PERSON (AS SHOWN ON SOCIAL SECURITY CARD)	Social security number of self-employed person
Joe Smith	120 30 3672

Business activities subject to self-employment tax (grocery store, restaurant, farm, etc.) ► *Manufacturing*

- If you have only farm income complete Parts I and III.
- If you have only nonfarm income complete Parts II and III.
- If you have both farm and nonfarm income complete Parts I, II, and III.

Part I Computation of Net Earnings from FARM Self-Employment **SE**

A farmer may elect to compute net farm earnings using the OPTIONAL METHOD, line 3, instead of using the Regular Method, line 2, if his gross profits are: (1) $2,400 or less, or (2) more than $2,400 and net profits are less than $1,600. However, lines 1 and 2 must be completed even if you elect to use the FARM OPTIONAL METHOD.

1 REGULAR METHOD—Net profit or (loss) from:
   (a) Schedule F, line 54 (cash method), or line 74 (accrual method) . . .
   (b) Farm partnerships . . . .
2 Net earnings from farm self-employment (add lines 1(a) and 1(b)) . . . .
3 FARM OPTIONAL METHOD—If gross profits from farming are: ¹

   (a) Not more than $2,400, enter two-thirds of the gross profits . . . . }
   (b) More than $2,400 and the net farm profit is less than $1,600, enter $1,600 . . . . . } . .
      ¹ Gross profits from farming are the total gross profits from Schedule F, line 28 (cash method),
      or line 72 (accrual method), plus the distributive share of gross profits from farm partnerships
      (Schedule K–1 (Form 1065), line 15) as explained in instructions for Schedule SE.

4 Enter here and on line 12(a), the amount on line 2, or line 3 if you elect the farm optional method .

Part II Computation of Net Earnings from NONFARM Self-Employment

5 REGULAR METHOD—Net profit or (loss) from:
   (a) Schedule C, line 21. (Enter combined amount if more than one business.) . . . . | 12,200 |
   (b) Partnerships, joint ventures, etc. (other than farming) . . . . | — |
   (c) Service as a minister, member of a religious order, or a Christian Science practitioner. (Include
      rental value of parsonage or rental allowance furnished.) If you filed Form 4361, check here ☐
      and enter zero on this line . . . . | — |
   (d) Service with a foreign government or international organization . . . . | — |
   (e) Other (director's fees, etc.). Specify ►... | — |
6 Total (add lines 5(a), 5(b), 5(c), 5(d), and 5(e)) . . . . | 12,200 |

7 Enter other adjustments (attach statement) . . . . | — |

8 Adjusted net earnings or (loss) from nonfarm self-employment (line 6, as adjusted by line 7) . . . | 12,200 |

If line 8 is $1,600 or more **OR** if you do not elect to use the Nonfarm Optional Method, omit lines 9 through 11 and enter amount from line 8 on line 12(b), Part III.

Note: You may use the nonfarm optional method (line 9 through line 11) only if line 8 is less than
$1,600 and less than two-thirds of your gross nonfarm profits,² and you had actual net earn-
ings from self-employment of $400 or more for at least 2 of the 3 following years: 1970, 1971,
and 1972. The nonfarm optional method can only be used for 5 taxable years.
      ² Gross profits from nonfarm business are the total of the gross profits from Schedule C, line 3,
      plus the distributive share of gross profits from nonfarm partnerships (Schedule K–1 (Form
      1065), line 15) as explained in instructions for Schedule SE. Also, include gross profits from
      services reported on lines 5(c), 5(d), and 5(e), as adjusted by line 7.

9 NONFARM OPTIONAL METHOD:
   (a) Maximum amount reportable, under both optional methods combined (farm and nonfarm) . . | $1,600 | 00 |
   (b) Enter amount from line 3. (If you did not elect to use the farm optional method, enter zero.) . .
   (c) Balance (subtract line 9(b) from line 9(a)) . . . .

10 Enter two-thirds of gross nonfarm profits ² or $1,600, whichever is smaller . . . .

11 Enter here and on line 12(b), the amount on line 9(c) or line 10, whichever is smaller . . . . .

99. This is the front of Schedule SE, a self employment tax return.

Part III   Computation of Social Security Self-Employment Tax

12 Net earnings or (loss):
    (a) From farming (from line 4) . . . .

    (b) From nonfarm (from line 8, or line 11 if you elect to use the Nonfarm Optional Method) . . . | 12,200 |
13 Total net earnings or (loss) from self-employment reported on line 12. (If line 13 is less than $400,
    you are not subject to self-employment tax. Do not fill in rest of form.) . . . . | 12,200 |
14 The largest amount of combined wages and self-employment earnings sub-
    ject to social security tax for 1973 is . . . . | $10,800 | 00 |

15 (a) Total "FICA" wages as indicated on Forms W-2 | — |
    (b) Unreported tips, if any, subject to FICA tax from
        Form 4137, line 9 . . . . | — |

    (c) Total of lines 15(a) and 15(b) . . . . | — |

16 Balance (subtract line 15(c) from line 14) . . . . | 10,800 |

17 Self-employment income—line 13 or 16, whichever is smaller . . . . | 10,800 |

18 If line 17 is $10,800, enter $864.00; if less, multiply the amount on line 17 by .08 . . . . . | 864 |
19 Railroad employee's and railroad employee representative's adjustment for hospital insurance bene-
    fits tax from Form 4469 . . . . | — |

20 Self-employment tax (subtract line 19 from line 18). Enter here and on Form 1040, line 55 . . . | 864 |

You may use this space to make any needed computations

100. The back of the Schedule SE.

FEDERAL INCOME TAXES   191

Name | Social Security Number

1   Enter amount of Adjusted Gross Income expected in 1973 (see note above Instruction 1) . . . . . .

      TAX TABLE USERS OMIT LINES 2 AND 3 AND ENTER TAX FROM TAX TABLE ON LINE 4

      (Caution: If another person is entitled to claim you as a dependent, see 1972 Instructions for Form 1040.)

2a If you expect to itemize deductions, enter estimated total of such deductions. If you do not expect to itemize deductions, enter 15% of line 1 (limited to $2,000 ($1,000 if married filing separately)) . . . . .

2b Exemptions ($750 for each, including additional exemptions for age and blindness) . . . .

3   Line 1 less the total of 2a and 2b. This is your estimated taxable income . . . .

4   Tax on amount on line 3 (see page 4 for tax rate schedules) . . . .

5   Tax from recomputing prior year investment credit (see Form 4255) . . . .

6   Estimate of 1973 self-employment income $_____ ; if $10,800 or more, enter $864.00; if less,
multiply the amount by .08. (If joint declaration and both have self-employed income, make separate
computations.) . . . .

7   Add lines 4, 5, and 6 . . . .

8   Credits { Retirement income credit, foreign tax credit, investment credit, credit for federal tax on gasoline, special fuels, and lubricating oil, political contributions, and work incentive program credit } . .

9   Line 7 less line 8 . . . .

10 Estimated income tax withheld and to be withheld during entire year 1973 . . . .

11 Estimated tax (line 9 less line 10). Enter here and in Block A on declaration–voucher. If $100 or more, file
the declaration–voucher. If less than $100, no declaration is required . . . .

12 Computation of installments:

| If declaration is due to be filed on: | { April 15, 1973, enter ¼
June 15, 1973, enter ⅓
September 15, 1973, enter ½
January 15, 1974, enter amount } | of line 11 here and on line 1 of original and subsequent declaration–vouchers } . . . . |

Note: *If your estimated tax should change during the year, you may use the amended computation below to
determine the amended amounts to be entered on declaration–voucher.*

Amended Computation			Record of Estimated Tax Payments				
(Use if estimated tax is substantially changed after the first decla-ration–voucher filed.)			Voucher number	Date (a)	Amount (b)	1972 overpayment credit applied to installment (c)	Total amount paid and credited from Jan. 1 through the installment date shown. Add (b), and (c) (d)
1 Amended estimated tax. (Enter here and in Block A on declaration–voucher.) . .			1				
2 Less:			2				
(a) Amount of last year's overpayment elected for credit to 1973 estimated tax and applied to date . . .			3				
(b) Payments made on 1973 declaration .			4				
(c) Total of lines 2(a) and 2(b)							
3 Unpaid balance (line 1 less line 2(c)) . .							
4 Amount to be paid (line 3 divided by num-ber of remaining installments). (Enter here and on line 1 of declaration–voucher.) . .			Total . . . . . ▶				

Detach here

---

101. Use this worksheet and 1040-ES voucher for figuring your estimated taxes for the following year.

STATE AND LOCAL TAXES

If you're subject to state or local income taxes, you'll probably be allowed to use the same figures for business profits or losses as filed on your federal income tax forms. Check with your state or local tax offices for information and forms required.

Your city or state may also require you to pay "Unincorporated Business Taxes." This means if your business makes a profit above a certain amount, you'll have to pay this tax in addition to personal income taxes. New York State at the present time allows a $5,000 deduction on net income with an unincorporated business tax on the balance of 5½%. Check with your city and state departments of taxation and finance to find out if your business is subject to such a tax.

HELP!

Yes, you may very well be justified in crying, "Help!" at tax time. We've tried to cover the basic taxes, forms, etc., but you'll be responsible for filing everything yourself. If you're used to doing your own taxes, enjoy pouring through the I.R.S. publications, and have your bookkeeping records in tip-top shape, maybe you can handle it yourself. But for many of you, a tax expert will be welcome somewhere between January 1st and April 15th. If you've already used an accountant to help set up your books, this is the person to see now. If not, try a personal recommendation or a recognized tax accounting organization in your town to get some assistance. The fee you pay will be an allowable expense on next year's return.

CHECKLIST

1. Compute business profit or loss on yearly income statement as shown in Chapter 7.

2. If your business is run on a cash basis, i.e., profit equals money taken in minus money spent, fill out Schedule C using the cash method.

3. If your business accounting is based on inventories, accounts receivable, depreciation, etc., complete Schedule C on the accrual basis.

4. Enter net profit or loss from Schedule C on line 28, Part I, of Form 1040. Business profits or losses will be added to or subtracted from your other earnings.

5. Fill in Schedule C-2 to show depreciation for any major machinery or equipment purchases.

6. If you earned wages less than $10,800 that were subject to social security taxes, you'll be required to pay self-employment taxes on business profits.

7. If you expect to make a profit the following year, file a Form 1040-ES (estimated taxes) by April 15th.

8. You may be subject to state or local income taxes, or unincorporated business taxes. See your local agencies for information.

9. It's very likely you'll want to consult a tax expert for assistance in figuring your taxes. The fee you pay will be an allowable expense on the following year's return.

18
YOUR BUSINESS AND YOU

"How's business?" a friend asks. A simple enough question. You could answer, "Fine," and let it go at that, or if your friend has a few hours you could begin to give him an idea of how the business really is. When someone asks this question a hundred things run through your mind. You think about the shipment of clasps or hooks or yarn that's three weeks late and how you'll pay for it when it arrives. You think about your best sales-person who hasn't sent in an order this week. You think about the price of that new machine and the space you'll need if you get it. You even worry about that big order you hope to get, because you can't fill it without more help, yet you can't hire anyone else until you get the order. And you think about giving up the whole thing and fleeing to South America.

You realize that there's no short answer to "How's business?" because by now the business is you and you are the business. You're so emotionally involved that a real answer is now as much an autobiography as a description of financial status. To separate out a list of facts about your business is like trying to describe a good dinner by telling someone the weight, mineral content, and density of each of the ingredients.

YOU AND YOUR FEELINGS

Your business reflects you — the way you think and feel, and at the same time it creates feelings and emotions within you. Your work affects your family and friends. It affects your social life, limits your time, and fills you with both frustration and satis-faction.

It takes a healthy personality to run a successful business (or even to lose one), and it takes healthy personalities to live with the businessperson. For example, if the boss is the wife, what happens to the cooking and housekeeping? Can a male chauvinist coexist with a female president? What about the children — should they be sent off to Aunt Laura's for the first two years? Can you invite friends into a house-full of leather, clay, wood, tools, and odd noises? And can you train your cat to stop dragging parts of your manu-facturing operation into the living room?

These are a few of the reasons you'll need a healthy personality. Some of the questions might be solved only after a small craft business run at home shows a decent profit. Then, you *could* move the business into a small building, have a cook, a maid, and a Nanny (who likes cats). But, even if you could afford it, solutions to such problems are rarely clear cut. Often, rather than being able to work these problems *out*, we've settled for continuously working *on* them, with all the compromises and conflicts that can result. We've come to live with a degree of uncertainty, risk, and ambiguity.

Risk and Uncertainty. Everyone makes decisions no matter how trivial or important. Shall I read the paper now or later? Should I take this job or that one? It's the same in your business. Should I make two more pots or twenty? Should I buy another loom? And the answers to the more important questions can and will affect your business — perhaps set you back a few thousand dollars or put you ahead as much. Decisions, life, and business all involve risk.

If you already know that you can cope with this rather normal human condition, then you're likely to run a successful business. Part of the challenge of business is that decisions count. You can't ignore a problem hoping it will go away. You're pulling a number of strings, running a fascinating, complex show, and all the parts have to fit together to make it work. You'll find yourself organizing, analyzing, and deciding all the time. It's stimulating, exciting, frustrating, and because of this it draws on all the strengths and talents you have.

Decision-Making. Can you look at an incomplete set of facts and still make a decision? Can you act wisely, with less than perfect information? We like to think of a decision as a mixture of both facts and feelings. For example, when buying a car you might settle on two similar models and make a final decision based on the color. You buy the blue one not because it will run better, but because you like the color blue. Here, as in many decisions, the facts alone aren't sufficient to make a decision. Your feelings, your values, and your opinions have to be added to the facts before a decision is made.

It's the same in business. You have two sample pieces of leather. Both cost the same and are the same quality, so the facts alone would allow you to toss a coin. But in dealing with the tanners, you happen to like tanner A better than tanner B, not because you know that A will deliver faster and will keep his price down or that B won't. It's just a feeling, an opinion, so you risk tanner A. And if you aren't right, few things are irrevocable; you can always switch to tanner B.

Or again, you're designing a new pot. Shall it be brown with a small mouth, or blue with a large mouth? Look around the gift shops and in the trade journals gathering as many facts as you can. Is brown really "in" this season as they contend? How many should you make? Should you also stock some of the blue ones? The facts as you can see, are limited. You'll really know only after the season is over. But you must decide now. What, after all your observations, do *you* think? How do *you* feel about it? Go with the one that has the most heart, that you like best. Stock some of the other also if you can, but act, decide, and risk, by adding your feelings to the facts. Decisions are part fact (and we hope this book has given you a firm foundation of factual business knowledge), part value system. Recall that it's your value system that produced the kind of craft you're in, the beauty of it, and the joy of it. Respect your own feelings, and listen to your values.

YOU AND YOUR FAMILY

As we've previously stated, a description of your business is much like an auto-biography. In a small business you're the boss, the accountant, the designer, the vice-president for sales, and a number of other titles. We've also mentioned that your time is now limited. Since you're concentrating on your business, what happens to your children and your mate? Is the business compatible with your other important values? Here again, we present a problem with no easy solution. We work on it as it comes up, hashing it out and rehashing it whenever we bump into another obstacle.

Problems often arise if there are children in the family, however, we have an outgoing, healthy daughter who at age six, has sufficient outside interests and friends to keep her busy most of the time. But not always. Sometimes children want to share the attention the business is getting. We've found that many children just naturally like to help, and so we've looked for a couple of little jobs, quite safe, that our daughter can do. Hair barrettes, for example, have dowels going through them that must be sharpened first to a dull point, and she is our best sharpener. She also does a fair job of tying tags onto the finished product. Incidentally, children will soon find other things to do, so don't count on the regular forty-hour week (or even two hours), and don't fret about their constantly being underfoot. They'll probably soon lose interest, but they'll know you've accepted them when they wanted to be with you, and that's all that counts, even if you lost $10.00 worth of production in the process. Of course there'll be times when you really can't be interrupted, but reason, love, and a promise to read a story later will usually be well-received.

It may be easier to deal with youngsters than adults. In our set-up, Lyn is president (and all the rest of the management functions) and Herb has a regular job, acting only as consultant to the craft business. Consultants advise and suggest, accept their fee and, typically, leave the scene. Husband-consultants, however, remain on the scene and like to see their suggestions acted on. But presidents don't always have the same value systems as consultants, just as no two people feel exactly the same way about things. Thus are the seeds of conflict sown. If, after all the facts are in, Herb says a particular design won't work, and Lyn says it will, a compromise won't solve the conflict. Here, as in many decisions, the sole proprietor frequently has to go it alone, taking the risk, the failures, and the successes in stride.

When both husband and wife are running the business, taking a back seat might not be so easy. One can dissolve a partnership and still run a thriving business, but marriage dissolving is quite another thing. There are alternatives — if running the business together is creating conflict and anger that reaches into the marriage relationship, one has to decide which is more important. Our value system says, "Let the partnership go well before the marriage." Another alternative is to allocate certain parts of the business to each mate. He may have strengths in design and production; she may be a whiz at sales, raising capital, and accounting. In this kind of set-up one mate persuades, suggests, and advises about the other's specialty, but final decisions rest with the one responsible for that function. Of course, decisions have to be well-integrated. He can't say, "we'll buy two new kilns," if she can't possibly expect to market the production or even get the loan for the purchase of the kilns. So argument, understanding, and perhaps some compromise will definitely go a long way.

Other Organizational Structures. Still another alternative is to add a prosperous partner. The third person may settle a tie vote or he may be "silent," but in either event he can be solicited for help and information. Often, the more ideas the better. We've all heard that "too many cooks spoil the pot," but in the planning and idea stages it often helps to get a number of ideas. In the same way, with or without a third partner, employees can contribute ideas. If you've hired people to help you, they'll have ideas about production, inventory, space, tools, and perhaps sales and even sources of money.

Naturally you'll set up your organization as seems best, according to size, capital, and talent. Each organization structure has advantages and disadvantages. The sole proprietor structure often allows for quicker decision-making, but perhaps it's not as well-planned or well-informed as the two-man or group structure.

TRY IT, YOU'LL LIKE IT

An important issue is the compatibility between your business and your feelings. If you're not yet in business and are contemplating it, we hope you'll decide to try it regardless of the risks. You and your family may find that the business will become a bond, a mutual interest, an exciting topic of conversation. If you're forewarned about the possible pitfalls and agree to go ahead with it, you'll be approaching it with a clear head. The challenge is exhilarating and will constantly test your wits and muscle as well as your maturity and ability to cope. Dreams and hopes for success pull you along; they help you overcome obstacles you never believed you could handle. If you're ready to grow and want to get the satisfaction that comes from accomplishment, why not take the plunge? When your business grows and becomes financially profitable, you'll get a double payoff — personal growth *and* profit.

BUSINESS CAN BE BEAUTIFUL

Your own business, as you can see, will be quite a challenge. It lives, and you live with it; in a fairly short time you can see the results of actions, your decisions. If you buy a new tool either it works or it doesn't. If you design a new vase, it sells or it doesn't. In any case, you learn something, you change and grow.

If you want to expand and take out a loan, you work it out on paper, scrape together as many numbers and quantifiable facts as possible, throw in a dash of pure intuition and hope, and plunge ahead. What you accomplish lifts you right off the ground. And your failures provide useful feedback for the next decision, the next risk.

Of course it's a risk. But risk doesn't mean your business will fail; it may also thrive. And there's you — your mind is a most fantastic device. Unlike a computer, it can deal not only with taxes and hours and money but with human qualities that make your decisions right. And when you've made a wrong turn, you can always change direction — few things are irrevocable.

Most important of all are your hopes and dreams. You want to make it work for profit and for your own growth. Our dreams have a marvelous ability to pull us forward, leveling all obstacles and causing us to hope, to act, and to grow. And you, in business or in anything, can have these hopes, can risk those actions, and can reap the rewards of growth and self-fulfillment. Success in your business, and have a good life.

BIBLIOGRAPHY

Agyris, Chris. *Integrating the Individual & the Organization.* New York: John Wiley & Sons, Inc., 1964.

Athos, Anthony, and Robert Coffey. *Behavior In Organizations: A Multidimensional View.* Englewood Cliffs, New Jersey: Prentice-Hall, 1968.

Drucker, Peter F. *The Practice of Management.* New York: Harper & Row, 1954.

Johnson, David W. *Reaching Out: Interpersonal Effectiveness and Self-Actualization.* Englewood Cliffs, New Jersey: Prentice-Hall, 1972.

Koontz, Harold, and Cyril O'Donnell. *Principles of Management,* 4th ed. New York: McGraw-Hill, 1968.

Lasser, J.K. *Your Income Tax.* New York: Simon & Schuster, 1973.

Pyle, William W., and John Arch White. *Fundamental Accounting Principles,* 6th ed. Homewood, Illinois: Richard D. Irwin, 1972.

Rogers, Carl. *On Becoming a Person.* Boston, Massachusetts: Houghton Mifflin, 1961.

Stanton, William J. *Fundamentals of Marketing,* 3rd ed. New York: McGraw-Hill, 1971.

Strauss, George and Leonard R. Sayles. *Personnel: The Human Problems of Management.* Englewood Cliffs, New Jersey: Prentice-Hall, 1972.

1973 U.S. Master Tax Guide. Chicago: Commerce Clearing House, 1973.

TRADE MAGAZINES

American Glass Review, 1115 Clifton Ave., Clifton, New Jersey 07013

American Jewelry Manufacturer, Biltmore Hotel, Suite S-75, Providence, Rhode Island 02902

Boutique Fashions, 50 Hunt St., Watertown, Massachusetts 02172

Ceramic Scope, 6363 Wilshire Blvd., Los Angeles, California 90048

Furniture Design & Manufacturing, 7373 N. Lincoln Ave., Chicago, Illinois 60646

Furniture Methods & Materials, P.O. Box 16528, Memphis, Tennessee 38116

Gifts & Decorative Accessories, 51 Madison Ave., New York, N.Y. 10010

Gift & Tableware Reporter, 165 W. 46th St., New York, N.Y. 10036

Glass Digest, 15 E. 40th St., New York, N.Y. 10016

Handbags & Accessories, 80 Lincoln Ave., Stamford, Connecticut 06904

Journal of the American Candlemaker, 2010 Sunset Dr., Pacific Grove, California 93950

Leather & Shoes, 2720 Des Plaines Ave., Des Plaines, Illinois 60018

Luggage & Leather Goods, 80 Lincoln Ave., Stamford, Connecticut 06904

Profitable Craft Merchandising, Pleasantville, New York 10570

Western Outfitters, 5314 Bingle Rd., Houston, Texas 77018

Woodworking & Furniture Digest, Hitchcock Bldg., Wheaton, Illinois 60187

Edited by Joan Fisher
Set in 10 point Press Roman by Black Inc.
Printed and bound by George Banta Co.